THE PENNSYLVANIA GHOST GUIDE
Vol. II

To Rosie, Never stop asking the questions. Patty A. W 5-4-02

Welcome to the world of author Patty A. Wilson and her friends. Ms. Wilson once again delivers a fantastic tour of Pennsylvania's most haunted sites. She and her friends not only visit some of the sites in the book, but they find the spirits and tell their stories through the use of a combination of scientific equipment and hard work.

Go to the U.S. Hotel in Blair County where the most active ghosts in Pennsylvania seem to live. Visit Gettysburg and listen to the tales of tourists who came away with unexpected stories of the spectral dead who still inhabit the old town. Hear the first-person account of a man who grew up in a haunted house in Brownsville, PA. And stop along the way to visit many other haunted sites that you have probably never heard of before!

Ms. Wilson has made a career of writing about Pennsylvania's wonderful and weird history. She writes for the *Shopper's Guide of Bedford and Blair Counties* and the *Altoona Mirror* in Blair County. Ms. Wilson also freelances and has now written three books--though she has another three on the way... She enjoys both traditional history and parapsychology and often blends the two in her work. Ms. Wilson began the Central Pennsylvania Paranormal Association about a year ago, and in this book she introduces the reader to both some of the participants and to their work.

Ms. Wilson lives in Martinsburg in Blair County and continues to collect odd stories for yet another volume in the chronicle of Pennsylvania's odd history.

Dr. Hans Holzer, the foremost parapsychologist in the field has written of Ms. Wilson's work, "Patty Wilson's authoritative book, *Haunted Pennsylvania*, is an excellent and entertaining work dealing with true cases of hauntings in the Keystone State. It deserves a place in any library, especially those containing major works in the field."

This book promises to be even more interesting and frightening than those that came before!

The Pennsylvania Ghost Guide Vol. II
Copyright (c) 2001, Patty A. Wilson

ISBN: 0-9700650-1-9

Cover and artwork copyright (c) 2001 Piney Creek Press

Cover design and Printing A$^+$ Printing, Inc. Altoona, PA
Cover photograph by Becky Gummo

All rights reserved. No part of this book, either in part or in whole, may be reproduced, transmitted or utilized in any form or by any means, electronic, photographic, or mechanical, including photocopying, recording, or by any information storage and retrieval system, without the permission in writing from the Publisher, except for brief quotations embodied in literary articles and reviews.

First Printing: May 2001

For permissions, or for serialization, condensation, or for adaptations, write the Publisher at the address below:

Piney Creek Press
P.O. Box 227
Roaring Spring, PA 16673
(814) 793-2260

Cover photograph of paranormal researcher Scott Crownover in a cemetery in Blair County, PA. Mr. Crownover was not holding any lighting instrument when this photo was taken. The light is called supercharged energy and was not seen by the naked eye at the time that the photograph was snapped. Insert photo is of Lillie Wright Showalter.

DEDICATION

Best friends are a special gift and a rarity in this life. They teach you about yourself and help you grow. They drag you along on their adventures and willingly share yours. Through the past two books I have found some dear friends. I dedicate this book to the Old Boot-- Al Brindza who is always there when we need him, and Becky Gummo who had held my hand and become my sister. And particularly to the one who has shared more adventures with me than anyone--a guy who isn't afraid to sit in a cemetery when it's "a bit nippy" at night--Scott Crownover. Thank you all for the life lessons you have each given me, and for your tireless help with this book. I think that together we make quite a team!

BEFORE YOU BEGIN READING:

Though I have tried to use the real names of people in the following stories, there are a few times when it has been requested that I use pseudonyms. When these appear, they will be printed as follows, *Terry Smith.

ACKNOWLEDGMENTS

Through the years I have come to understand that every book is actually a cooperative effort between not only the publisher and writer, but the friends of the writer as well. This book would not have been possible without the dedication, support and research abilities of several folks.

Al Brindza has cheered me on and offered advice throughout the entire book writing process. He has become my number one salesman, and one of the best paranormal investigators I have ever had the pleasure of working with. His meticulous nature and exacting standards have raised the bar for everyone in paranormal research.

Scott Crownover has brought his scientific interests into the field of paranormal research. He came to us a novice, but quickly showed not only his aptitude for this field of research, but his dedication to excellence as well. Through this past year Scott has became one of the best investigators anywhere. His honest and enthusiastic approach has been refreshing to see. And he has been my sounding board and my proof reader as well.

Becky Gummo has been my constant friend for two years and co-creator of the Central Pennsylvania Paranormal Association. Together we have worked our way through many stories, but Becky will always like to quietly go off and take her photos. She, too, has taught me a great deal about this field.

I want to thank the rest of the group who have so kindly shared their interests. They have helped me in so many ways.

And there have been others who have shared their stories and offered me their support. I thank each of you who so patiently explained about your haunted experiences and who allowed me into your lives. I have felt honored to share this part of your life with you.

I want to thank the folks at the many historical societies who have so painstakingly helped me with research, and often for no more than a smile and a "thank you." You folks are underestimated and appreciated in this world. Thanks for all of the help!

If I have forgotten anyone, please forgive me for it is not intentional. As you can see, this book is not the endeavor of a single person, but the result of many kind folks who have shared their time, knowledge and lives with me so that I could share them with you.

Patty A. Wilson

Patty A. Wilson

TABLE OF CONTENTS

THE U.S. HOTEL

(Hollidaysburg, Blair County)

I have been fortunate enough to have good friends who not only root out potential ghost stories for me, but who then want to help investigate the haunting as well. Scott Crownover is such a friend. He has spent countless hours searching out stories, and then helping research them. He was the one who found out that the U.S. Hotel in Hollidaysburg is haunted. He then made arrangements for several friends and I to spend the night in the building. Together we came away with more stories than we ever bargained for, and I finally had my first truly frightening experience.

In the early 1800s Hollidaysburg, PA was a thriving little town. It was named for Adam Holliday who settled there after the Revolutionary War. Holliday laid out the town and worked hard to promote it. With the completion of the Pennsylvania Canal, Hollidaysburg became a town of importance. The canal built on the Juniata River opened a trade route to the east. The need for hotels and taverns to house the ever-increasing traffic brought by the canal did not escape John Dougherty who built the U.S. Hotel that same year. He capitalized upon the westward travelers heading into the untamed Wild West.

The U.S. Hotel was a lovely building that offered lodgings, food and drink for those so inclined. It sat right along the Juniata Basin among the warehouses and wharfs that had grown up along with the ever-growing canal. It was noted that by 1837 the canal had fourteen daily boats off-loading and on-loading from this area and the U.S. Hotel sat right at the edge of all of this. It was a grand lady along the wharf.

Dougherty found that his business was growing. He married and had a child during those years. His dreams were destroyed, though, by a fire on Nov. 29, 1871. The fire destroyed much of the hotel. Dougherty did not rebuild his grand hotel. Instead, he sold the building to a German immigrant named Engelbert Gromiller in 1886. Gromiller rebuilt the hotel that stands to this day. He added a brewery in an adjoining building that had once housed mules. Gromiller was a brew master by trade in his homeland of Bavaria, and he continued this trade in Hollidaysburg. He served his masterfully brewed ale in the hotel and he picked up the trade again.

By this time, the canals had faded into the mists of history, but between the old canal and the U.S. Hotel now ran the railroad tracks. Where once the warehouses had housed goods off-loaded from the canal boats, they now housed goods offloaded from trains. The tide of those immigrating westward was still growing and Gromiller's hotel earned a reputation as "the best $1.50 a day house in the borough."

Along with the trade that came from being a popular establishment came all sorts of folks. The hotel housed families, businessmen and all manners of business people.

A bar was added to the building in 1905 and is still much as it was designed by the then owner. The brewery is long gone, but where it stood there is now empty an empty lot that will be built upon this year. Much of the history of the hotel's early days still exists for those who wish to enjoy it. From the grand pillars and high, classic ceilings to the hand-carved mahogany back bar and silvered beveled mirrors in the bar, the former grandeur is apparent.

In 1945 the building was used as a radio school for the United States Navy during World War II. The bar was dismantled and stowed and the room was used as a shower. The kitchen became a mess and the dining rooms were used for offices, schoolrooms and meals. Upstairs, the once lovely bedrooms were turned over to a grimmer customer. Young men who would soon be on battlefields and in field offices spent their final peaceful nights there. Who is to say what residual effect this time left upon the hotel? Many of the young men who trained there would go on to die upon anonymous battlefields, and perhaps they longed for the "good times" when they were back in school.

After the government was through with the building in 1945, the Gromiller family decided to reassemble the bar room and put the building up for sale. Through the years, the building changed hands several times. Some owners were kind and cared for the building to the best of their ability, while others allowed it to decline. The brewery was destroyed and the once grand hotel grew sad and tired. However, a reprieve was given to the hotel in 1994 when the Yoders purchased the building. They saw the former grandeur still within the walls, but hidden by the debris of careless ownership. The family set about carefully resurrecting the building and restoring it to it's former beauty. Now the downstairs is once more graceful. The original bar room is now a dining area and the original kitchen has become a smaller dining room. The building is still changing, still evolving, and the Yoders are carefully, lovingly orchestrating this rebirth.

When they were first approached about the possibility of ghosts in their restaurant, Karen Yoder was kind and receptive. This was not the first time that she had heard the stories. The old kitchen was long believed to be home to "Sarah" a female spirit who liked to play little tricks upon the staff. Several staff members had spoken of sitting down glasses to have them spill and of plates suddenly swept to the floor though no one was near.

Karen's adult son, Jason, told of an incident that occurred when he was working upon the remodeling of the small back dining room. The bar closed at 2 a.m. and he had gone back to work on the painting of that room for a while. As he worked, he suddenly became aware of voices laughing and footsteps above him on the next floor. Jason knew that he was alone in the building, so "I just laid the paintbrush down and quietly left." He was not curious as to who was having such a good time above him because he knew that whoever they were, they were not alive.

Upstairs Karen knew of one incident with a female spirit who had watched a man who had spent the night in the building. Karen graciously invited us to come in and spend the night in the old hotel.

It was a cold night when we first arrived at the U.S. Hotel. Scott Crownover had found this site for us and he had told us about the main haunting. The owners Joe, Karen and Jason Yoder had told him that years earlier a workman, who was helping them redo some of the rooms, had an odd experience. The fellow had to drive a long way home each night, so Karen suggested that they set up a cot in the room that would eventually become the second floor office for this fellow.

The man met Karen at the door the next morning and said he'd be driving back and forth after all. "Why," Karen wanted to know. The man seemed shaken. He told her that around three a.m. he had awakened, but he couldn't tell why. While he was laying there listening to the darkness, something moved in the doorway and he turned in that direction. Hovering above the floor was a woman in a white dress or nightgown. She was just watching him. The man was visibly shaken by this woman, but the part that seemed to upset him the most was the fact that he insisted that the woman hovered 18 inches off the floor and she had no feet!

With that story in mind, Karen left us to our work--or should I say our fun? It would, however, turn out much differently than I had ever imagined.

For a while we wandered the building, getting the feel of the place. We split up into groups of twos because the building is large with two corridors of rooms on the second floor and as many more above that yet. I was with a friend named Al Brindza who is very sensitive to ghostly phenomena. Scott had partnered up with a friend of his named Stacie, and there was one other group that consisted of a young woman named Janelle and another friend of Scott's named Mike.

As we walked about, it was decided that it would be best if we each took an area and stayed put. First, Janelle and Mike entered the parlor or private dining area just to the right of the stairs. Behind Janelle was Stacie. As they opened the door to that room, they all three heard a deep female sigh from within that area. Then there was silence.

After that, Scott walked us through the second floor so that we could get the feel for the place before we set off on our own.

Al and I went down the first hall for a little while, but found nothing there. Janelle and Mike took the office where the woman in white was once seen. Stacie and Scott stepped through the door into the second hallway where the more derelict bedrooms were.

After a few moments, we suddenly heard a sound that caught our attention. It was a woman's voice, very excited or upset and it was coming from where Stacie and Scott had been. Quickly Al and I hurried into that area. Stacie met us near the door. She was running fast while Scott was trying to keep up with her. She looked terribly frightened and was repeating the words; "I gotta get out of here" over and over. She brushed past us and made for the stairs. For a brief second Scott stopped.

"What happened?" we asked.

Scott pointed down the hall to the left. "Down there. We got near that room and suddenly she just took off. She said she was feeling scared but..." He looked toward the door and shook his head. "This isn't like her."

He took off after her and Al and I were left to look down that hallway. Now I've never been afraid of anything like ghosts or old houses or empty rooms. At that time, I did not know Stacie, so I had no way to judge the seriousness of what she was experiencing. I would later learn that she's not an easily rattled woman.

Al and I made our way down the hall. At the doorway of that bedroom, we paused. There was a distinct change in the atmosphere. It was alive, electric and so cold that I was shivering. Al tried to snap a picture in that room, but his camera malfunctioned. Immediately I snapped a camera shot into the room just in case there was something there. I had no real hope of finding anything. I've often taken photos like that before, but in that one camera flash my whole perspective on ghosts and hauntings would suddenly change.

I saw a pretty woman with long auburn hair lying on a bed in that room. She was covered with a light brown or tan blanket and I could see what appeared to be a slip she was wearing. She was writhing in pain and holding her head. As suddenly as I caught this glimpse, she was gone in the darkness after the flash. I had this sudden intense fear and a sense of terrible pain and the word "Run!" kept screaming in my head.

Now I've never had a psychic experience in my life. I turned away toward a window and light and began quietly talking to myself. I was fighting for composure; for a way to make sense of the impossible thing my eyes just told my mind I had seen.

Al had been looking into the room, too, and now he looked at me and he was pale, sick in the half-light. "You saw her, too." It was not a question, but a statement. My own shocked eyes met his. I had never been so grateful in my life for a friend. This man had

3

witnessed what I had; only more intensely I would come to learn.

I nodded in response to his statement and he simply said. "She was in a lot of pain. She was really hurt." I would not know until later that though we saw the same woman, and I saw her holding her head and writhing in pain, Al would see what was causing the pain. The woman had slashes across her body.

We had asked for an experience by ghost hunting so we knew that we had to continue with our investigation. Al and I walked into the bedroom, but there was no one there now. It was still very cold in the room and the electric feeling was strong, but we walked through this bedroom to the adjoining hall on the other side. As we looked around a bit, we both caught a quick glimpse of a black shadow running down the hall and disappearing around a corner. Quickly we verified that we both had seen the same thing as we hurried after it.

At the end of the hall there was a large room and beyond that a doorway leading down into the darkness. Al made it as far as the door before he stepped back. *Stairs where orbs, a black shadow and EVP* "Whatever's here is down there," he indi- *have been found.* cated the doorway. "I can't go down there."

We turned back and had barely regained the bedroom where we had seen the woman when Scott's voice called us back to where we had stood when I had snapped that photo. This area is a sort of landing where one could enter the bedroom and hall beyond or turn up the stairs, or even back into a parlor. Stacie was shaken, but she had come back to join us.

Now we conferred about what to do next. Al was still standing before that bedroom looking into it from time to time. Something there was bothering him. Yet we had all decided to examine the next level of the building.

Scott led the way up the stairs, Stacie followed him and I followed her. Al still hesitated outside the bedroom. He wanted to take another photo of the room. Suddenly Al's voice cut through the darkness. "Everyone out of here now." The sound of his voice instantly told me how serious the situation was. The others on the stairs heard the command and knew we had to obey. Quickly we hurried out of the hall. Al and Stacie continued down the stairs while Scott and I retrieved the others on that floor. We did not know what the danger was, but the sound of Al's voice brooked no less than total obedience.

Downstairs once more the group split up. Stacie was sitting and trying to calm down. Al was gone and Scott and I began looking for him. He was pacing the hallway between the kitchen and bar holding his stomach. He could not talk, and waved us away when we tried to help him. He went toward the bar where Scott would find him slumped against a wall in the bathroom. He was physically ill.

There was nothing that Scott or I could do to help Al except to allow him some time, so we returned to the main group. Each of them were talking, telling of their experiences-everyone except for Stacie. Her eyes were big and shadowed with fear. Stacie is a very pretty woman and now her pale complexion and the fear in her eyes made her look so young and vulnerable. I was worried about her. When she finally spoke, her voice was quiet, soft with the emotions she had felt. She told us that the first time she had been in that area something had just felt like it was all around her and she had to get away from it.

At last, Al returned to us and he too looked pale, tired and vulnerable. He struggled for the words to tell us what had happened. He was very shaken. At length he managed to tell us that while we were starting up the stairs he had hesitated at the doorway of that bedroom because he had hoped for another photo of the room. Suddenly in the doorway directly opposite him there was this black shadow of a man. The shadow had been carrying what appeared to be an ax and Al suddenly understood that this man was responsible for the slashed woman we had seen earlier. This man had been horrifying in his anger and hatred. I'd known Al long enough to know that he's not prone to imagining things and often doubts his own perceptions. If he was so sure of what he saw that he ordered us away, he saw that black shadow man.

Now began our hunt for information about the building. We had been told of the woman who floated in the first hallway and of "Sarah" on the first floor. No one knew anything about them or even if it was only one woman haunting both areas. There was no real reason for the name of Sarah, it was just a tag given to the spirit by a waitress years earlier, and it had stuck. Sometimes folks will name their ghosts as a way of dealing with them and it seems to help.

We had also been told about the mysterious behavior of a locked liquor cabinet in the main first floor hall. Karen reported that though she always checked that cabinet to be sure it was locked when she closed up, she had come in a few times to find the door wide open. However, no liquor had ever been removed. She couldn't explain these episodes.

We were also told about the mysterious picture in the bar. Hanging at the back of the bar is a photograph of the U.S. Hotel around the turn of the century. In the foreground are

a man and a woman holding a child. The man appears to be James Gromiller and that would make the woman his wife and child logically. The Yoders had the photograph taken down in order for it to be copied and printed on post cards and placemats. The placemats and postcards are an exact replica of the photograph with one exception. In the reproductions the woman is no longer holding a

U.S. Hotel postcard courtesy of the Yoders.

baby. It is as if the child just faded away. The Yoders asked the printer about it, but he denied altering the photograph in any way. Why should he take the trouble to do so unless they had requested it and why would they have done that? No one can explain the mystery of why the baby did not transfer over onto the print. It is clearly there in the original, and if you take a photograph of the original you will clearly see the child.

Now, though, we were faced with a real dilemma. Our experiences far exceeded anything that was in the recorded history. Now I am a careful person when it comes to such things. I want the truth only and I must say that despite my

The disappearing baby. Photo supplied by Scott Crownover.

5

best efforts I can find no verification for such a sensational crime. Of course, I must also add that the information on the hotel in the local archives is very sketchy. They offer only a brief biography of the owners and nothing more. Much of the rest of the history of building has only remained alive because of the owners and their desire to learn more about the building they have invested so much in.

One of the problems that we encountered was that we have virtually no time frame for this murder--if it ever really did happen. The only point of reference we had was the type of slip the young woman was wearing. It was from around 1900 in style. Of course, that does not mean very much. It is possible that she was wearing something out of style or that it was not really a slip but a filmy nightgown based on a popular design. It would literally take years of research through the newspaper archives to find any proof one way or the other. You would think that such an important event, if it were true would have come down in the oral history of the building, but it did not.

The only oral stories associated with it were that at one time a couple prostitutes used to work out of the hotel. This would not be surprising, as it was a bustling hotel in a wharf district. The hotel catered to all sorts and it would not be a large leap of logic to think that at least a few prostitutes plied their trade there through the years.

I have always maintained that I have no psychic ability and I really don't. However, when Scott, Mike and I returned to that bedroom to check it out again, I felt a terrible war going on in my head. At one point I had to stop because I had lost my equilibrium due to the confusion. I felt strongly that this woman had been a prostitute and that this man hated her for it. I kept hearing two voices in my head. A woman kept screaming "Run!" I felt like she was trying to protect me. Another voice was lower, deeper, a male voice and he kept muttering to himself, "I'll teach that bitch!" Now these impressions, and that's all they were, came before I knew about the possible prostitutes.

Another oddity surfaced that night, too. Al and I had seen that black shadow dash down the hall and down the stairs into a small room with no outside exit. Here we became confused because we thought he would stay in the building, but we both felt like he was reliving his escape. Later Scott would tell us that that room was originally an entrance to a courtyard, and that a person could very well have exited the building and escaped that way. Once more our perceptions were possible despite the physical evidence of the present.

Another anomaly of this haunting confused me even further. On the first floor, where the restaurant is, the feeling is good and safe. You don't feel any fear or unpleasantness at all. In fact, it is just the opposite. The building is lovely and you feel almost like you are stepping into another time. It is a lovely place to eat and the Yoders have given the restaurant a gracious atmosphere. So how could they have not noticed this other haunting that was so bad?

The answer may be that no one spends much time in that part of the building. It is virtually closed up. No one in the public goes there and the owners are only there to store or retrieve something. No one has slept in that room in many years.

Scott would find out that a previous owner had a son-in-law who had an experience on the third floor that had so frightened him that the man would not talk about what had happened to him. Unfortunately, just before we tracked the man down, he passed away. He had refused to talk about the experience with anyone. At least this was possible conformation that someone else had had an unpleasant experience in that part of the building.

After that first visit, the three of us who had experiences in that bedroom would all report nightmares. Amazingly, Al's dreams and mine were similar and featured the same young woman whom we had seen in that bedroom. Al's dreams were so bad that he awoke crying out. The dreams were about a woman who was hurt and about a fire. At this time, we still did not know that the U.S. Hotel had once burned down.

I dreamed of the woman's death. I heard her screams and I awoke sweating, frightened and feeling watched. It was so bad that I couldn't bear to be left alone at night for four nights.

Stacie also had horrible nightmares and after one such dream, she sat straight up in bed and grabbed at the light. As she flicked it on, she saw a black shadow flit through her room. She was terrified. She has not returned to the U.S. Hotel since that first night.

Al and Scott would make a daytime visit to the building and they came away with another interesting story to tell. First, they caught an orb in a photo in the back dining room. This was in the same spot where Al had felt a woman was sitting during our visit the prior week. He had picked up some orb photos in that room on that night, too. Al would later write of that visit, "...I went upstairs to the 2nd floor with Scott to check out that room again. Scott was ahead of me, already in the room when I entered the hallway and then I heard a 'Gasp!' And several words after that. I couldn't make out what they were. When I reached Scott and asked if he had heard that, he said no, but that it was here that Stacie freaked out. I was kind of hesitating about going near that room and I shouldn't have..."

"Anyway, Scott had the light on and we both felt how very cold it was in there. Then the pull chain on the ceiling light started moving. Get this! It moved from left to center, then back. Not left to center then right to center back to left! We both saw this. It was like something was keeping the chain from going full cycle."

"I also started feeling very hostile and restless in the few minutes I was in there and later, very sad and depressed. I had enough and we went back downstairs. I also felt a sharp pain in the lower right side of my back while near that room. I'm kind of sorry that I went back in there. In just that short time my mood changed 180 degrees.... I feel very tired now." He would report more bad dreams, too.

Al would often suffer headaches, sharp pains, dizziness, and angry mood swings in that area along with a terrible tiredness that is debilitating. That area literally drained him of energy. I usually don't have that drained feeling, but twice I've come home and slept all day because I felt so bad.

Of course, such experiences could not be dropped and the Yoders kindly allowed us to return to the building for another night. This time, though the feelings in the room were bad, they were not as intense as the first time. We decided to run tape players this time, but we didn't really hope for much. I've tried to record ghosts before but with little luck.

As we all explored the building once more, my friend Becky and I were on the third floor after spending some time in that bedroom. We were talking to Scott and Jason, Janelle's husband when we heard cries from the foot of the stairs. We hurried downward thinking that something bad had happened. Al was leaning against the door in that little landing or hallway where he had been standing when he had seen the black shadow on a previous visit. He looked a bit confused and disoriented and we recognized the signs that something paranormal was happening to him. He needed to get out of that area for a while.

Al decided to go up to the third floor and I knew he'd be safer up there because Scott understood what was happening and could help him if necessary. Later, Al would find a male voice on his cassette tape that had been running in his breast pocket when he mounted the stairs. The voice seemed to be gloating, "Scared them...Scared." it said.

Upstairs Scott was picking up anomalous readings with his electromagnetic field detector (EMF). Al tried to take a photo of that area with his digital camera, but nothing came out. He told Scott that he did not get anything. Here a male voice once again appeared on his tape. "In the shower, buddy," it said. They were standing in a bathroom when this happened. Now we knew that this fellow is interactive.

Downstairs both Al and I had our cassette recorders running in the small back dining room where there has been activity and we both picked up a woman saying, "Mary." Was

that the real name of the woman tagged as Sarah by a waitress long ago?

As the members of the group began to disperse in the wee hours of the morning, Scott and Jason and Janelle decided to spend the entire night. Jason and Scott did a tour of the upstairs around three a.m. and found that the light in the little parlor or dining area on the second floor just to the right as you top the steps was on. They turned it off on the way back down-

Phantom images that appear in this booth.
Photo by Scott Crownover

stairs. When they did their next circuit a while later, the light was once again on. This certainly was odd because they had been together the entire time! Who had turned on the light inside the locked building?

On our next visit Al would confine himself to the areas of the second floor where he was not near that room. He found little activity in the first hallway area, but when he finally ventured as far as the near end of the hallway things changed. He was running his camera with night vision while a group of us stood around him and talked. Suddenly a black flash passed us. "Did you see that?" Al excitedly quizzed. We all saw it. Becky's husband insisted that someone had touched his beard!

"Well at least this time we have that guy on tape," I said. Al looked at his camera and back at me.

"No, we don't," he said holding the camera out slightly. "He turned it off." Whatever or whoever that black flash had been had turned off the camera as it passed. That was why it had touched Ed's beard. It was reaching past him and turning off the camera on his way through.

After this night, we returned to the hotel for a brunch meeting of the Central Pennsylvania Paranormal

Upstairs of U.S. Hotel

Association. It was a lovely meal and we enjoyed the visiting that always occurs when we get together. After lunch, however, Scott and Al led the group upstairs for a tour. We've done such things at many other buildings, but rarely with such dramatic consequences.

Scott wrote a report of the events after the brunch for the CPPA journal and I'll reprint it here:

"...The meeting got started about 1p.m. A short history of the hotel and a discussion of the events we experienced there followed lunch. Patty related the things that have happened there last month, so I won't repeat them here. After lunch, Karen allowed us to take a tour of the hotel. The second and third floors are normally closed to the public, but exceptions can be made.

It turned out that some unusual things did happen that afternoon. I had a strange photo in the bedroom at the end of the hall. The room and doorframe are in perfect focus, but everything in the doorway is blurred. I wasn't the only one to have strange things happen to them. Many of you expressed a feeling of something odd, sinister on the second and third floors. For instance:

-Mary Foor had camera problems in the parlor on the second floor and in the room at the end of the far hallway that leads to the old office.

-An EMF of 4 mG was detected in the same bedroom where I took the strange photo.

-Kelly (Annette's friend) had a hard time breathing in the far hallway just outside of the strange bedroom.

-Al was getting an instant headache in the same area.

-Carolyn and Patty felt a breeze pass them twice in this same area, but could not locate the source.

-Another member felt a strong sensation of anxiety at the top of the stairs just outside the parlor.

-Darlene had camera problems in the bathroom on the second floor. In fact, the camera mysteriously turned itself off. This was very near where Al had his video camera turn itself off on a previous visit.

-Darlene had trouble taking a photo in the dining room where we ate after the meeting broke up.

-Another member reported feeling creepy in the bathroom there.

-Jo had a strange feeling in the ladies' room on the third floor.

-Patty had her camera fail in the ladies room.

-A woman in the bar expressed to us that she felt as if she was being watched in the main bathroom on the first floor. Subsequently there was some trouble taking a photo in there.

It seemed as if all the bathrooms in this place were very busy that day.

-We were fortunate that Annette had a cassette running upstairs. She picked up some interesting EVP on the second floor as she was ascending to the third floor.

There are probably more events that happened that afternoon, but I am not aware of them.

Something definitely inhabits the U.S. Hotel. We have had far too much happen to us during our visits for it all to be just coincidental.

I would like to thank Karen for opening up the hotel to us. Her generosity with the building has been fantastic."

After that meeting one of the group, Annette, brought us a cassette tape she had let run during the tour. As she was going up the stairs to the third floor--the same area outside that bedroom where so much else had happened, you can hear a man's voice call after her, "I'm here! Come on! Come on! Come on! Here's your nightmare!" (It could be "Enjoy your nightmare," that bit is slightly garbled.)

Whatever is at the U.S. Hotel is certainly bold and likes to bait young women. We have no explanations, only questions and a story like this one really has no ending. The entity confines itself to the second and third floors, at least in our experiences to date. He is not used to getting too much attention, but he thrives on it when he gets the chance. He will drain batteries and people for the energy to manifest and he's bold. However, I recommend that you stop by the U.S. Hotel for the atmosphere of the first floor; it is ingratiating and you'll have a fine meal. Check out the photograph in the bar and perhaps you'll even have an encounter with "Mary" or "Sarah." She's a most respectful spirit and you'll just love the atmosphere that the Yoders have worked so hard to create. Oh, and if you just happen to have an experience, well isn't that part of the fun, too?

I, like Scott, would like to offer Joe, Karen and Jason Yoder my heartfelt thanks! You have a lovely restaurant and a very active haunting. I greatly appreciate your sharing the story and your lovely building with us all.

INDIAN CROSSING

(Graceville, Bedford County)

I am often surprised by how people deal with their haunted homes. When I spoke to a woman I'll call *Karen on the phone, she was very blasé about her ghost. In fact, since she had lived in her home for many years, she no longer paid this annual visitor any attention at all.

"I've had many experiences," *Karen confided to me over the phone. This was the third time we'd talked, and Karen had a lot of experiences to relate. She hesitated for a second, "I'm not psychic," she said, "but I sometimes know things. I have always had this ability and I've been able to warn my family about bad things that are going to happen. I've also always been able to experience ghosts better than most people." She went on to relate how as a child she had experienced two hauntings in homes her family had rented. Each time no one else had experienced anything, but in the first house a family friend confirmed that what the child was saying was accurate. In the second case, she thought her own mother knew more than she ever said. Her mother had developed a hatred of a particular bedroom in the house and refused to even use it for storage.

Though Karen had called me for other reasons, she ended up telling me yet another of her experiences. She casually said to me, "Have I ever mentioned to you about the Indian who walks around here either every spring or fall? I don't remember which. Anyhow, he always comes from south to north and I've seen him passing the house for years. It's odd, though, that I don't ever see him going back."

I was not sure if she meant an old Indian man who was real or what. I asked her who he was and exactly what she meant.

"I don't know exactly who he is" she said, "but he's a ghost. I see him going along every year, and like I said, I'm not sure if it's spring or fall. I'll find out soon though, since spring is coming. He seems in a hurry and is headed north."

I wanted to know more. "What did this fellow look like?"

"You know," she hesitated, "That's sort of odd. I only ever catch glimpses of him. He's like a shadow out of the corner of my eye or something. He's just there and gone. I never can remember what he looked like, but I just know he's Indian and I've always felt that he was going to Battleground Hollow. You know I grew up in a house back there and they say that way back in history there was a massacre and encampment back there. I've just always connected him with that for some reason, I guess because if he keeps walking the way he is going he'd end up right there. Now when I was little my Daddy used to walk around Battleground Hollow collecting up arrowheads and stuff. He had cigar boxes full of them. I guess there was truth to that story. The area has always been called that and they even put a road sign up not long ago."

I asked her some questions about Battleground Hollow, but she knew very little actual history. I would later learn that Battleground Hollow had earned its name because of a battle between whites and the natives upon that spot.

Before she was done with her call, though, Karen mentioned just one more thing. "You know, I'd probably not have mentioned that Indian ghost if it hadn't been for my daughter. I told her about you and your books and that I was going to call you. She asked me why and I kind of hesitated because I didn't want anyone making fun of me. Then she surprised me by saying, 'Well don't forget to tell her about the Indian around here.'"

Karen was quite surprised that her daughter had even known about the Indian. She asked her daughter, now an adult woman with children of her own, how long she had known about the Indian and why she had never said anything.

Her daughter just shrugged, "I've always known he was here. I've seen him lots of times. It never dawned on me to mention him to anyone. He's just here."

Apparently Karen's daughter has inherited her mother's calm attitude toward hauntings.

Is this Indian repeatedly making the last trek of his life to Battleground Hollow for a long fought fight? It would be impossible to answer that question, but Karen will always believe that this Indian is returning annually to the battle where he died.

THE ANGRY MAN

(Blair County)

In my next book you will encounter Becky M. and her experiences with a demon as a child, but when I first met Becky she had more immediate concerns. You see she wrote to me to tell me that her four year old son *Michael was apparently experiencing a nasty haunting in their home. In fact, the little boy was terrified of this entity. Becky asked me if I would come to her home to investigate the house and offer her my opinion about this ghost. She was worried that perhaps this entity might hurt her little son.

I asked three friends, Becky Gummo, Al Brindza and Scott Crownover to come along. Now I have worked with these folks many times and I value their dedication and opinions very much. Scott tends to look for validation through his equipment. In fact, in nearly every photo of Scott I have, his electromagnetic field detector and thermal probe are glued to his hands.

Al Brindza is sensitive to ghosts. Something about them makes him feel light-headed and dizzy. He also can see spirits that others do not see. I find this interesting, particularly as he describes these things to me and I can document that such people did inhabit many of the places he is talking about. When Al tells me something, I listen intently as he is very often right. He has good judgment and a drive to verify and document what he senses in a way that we can all experience. For that reason he has spent a lot of money on night vision cameras and other equipment so that he can capture many of his experiences for others to share. I have to say that Al has been amazingly successful at this.

Becky Gummo you are probably familiar with if you read the first Ghost Guide. Becky shies away from calling herself "sensitive," but she does seem to have a real gift for capturing spirits on film. She also senses that they are present when others seem unaware and her intuitions are most often accurate. I have come to trust her judgments about haunted houses.

It was a beautiful late September evening when we all arrived at Becky M.'s home between Williamsburg and Martinsburg, in Blair County. Becky M. and a friend, *Christine were waiting for us. Christine had been a friend of Becky M.'s husband, *Robert before Becky and Robert had gotten together. In fact, Christine had helped Robert move into the house nearly nine years ago, and she had experienced the unnerving feeling of being watched or of invading someone else's space long before Becky M. had arrived. Since then, Christine has become a good friend to Becky M. and Becky M. has confided the many little instances of haunting that make up a truly haunted house.

While we were all sitting around talking, I asked Becky M., who was standing by the sink, if she could repeat the stories she had told me for the entire group. Al and Scott knew nothing about Becky M.'s conversations. (I also ask folks to repeat stories to see if they might change them, and also because when folks are nervous they often forget critical details that only are remembered upon retelling.)

Becky M. began to talk and Al started walking around taking a few photos as he went. Scott quickly unpacked his equipment and began to run the EMF meter around the room. Almost immediately he found a field of electrical disturbance near the left side of Becky M. Now Scott quickly ascertained where the electrical wiring for the house was and took the readings of those outlets in the area. The readings were much different and none of them extended anywhere near far enough to effect where Becky M. was standing. Scott again played the equipment over the area of her side when suddenly the electrical field shifted to Becky M.'s right side. Puzzled now, Scott moved to the right side and picked up the readings only briefly as the field once again shifted to her left. Now Scott picked up his thermal scanner and ran it over the area of electrical disturbance. The temperature dropped by nearly 4 degrees. Scott found that he lost the field at about the three-foot height, and that there was no logical reason for the temperature drop and the floating field.

Al was watching this curiously and suddenly he cleared his throat. "Do you have like a little girl who haunts here?" he asked softly.

Becky M. looked at him sharply. "I know that this will sound crazy, but sometimes I used to sense a little girl down here." She indicated the kitchen. "I don't feel her very much anymore, but I used to. I just chalked it up to imagination, though, when Michael never mentioned seeing her."

"You have a little girl haunting down here," Al stated simply. "She's about four and she's shy."

Becky Gummo and I looked at each other. I knew exactly what Scott was picking on his EMF and why it was moving now. Every mother in the world has experienced a child hiding behind them and dancing from side to side to see something that has them curious, but that they are too shy to leave mom to look at. For a little while Scott kept moving his equipment over Becky M. and repeatedly the field would shift from side to side away from Scott. Becky M. kept insisting that she could feel the coldness encircle her leg as the field moved. At one point Scott lost the field entirely and he stood back. "I guess it's gone," he said, running the equipment across the room.

Becky M. just smiled nervously. "I think she's behind me. I can feel her little hand on my inside leg." Becky M. leaned forward slightly and Scott picked up the EMF field between her and the sink. Al came up with an idea to help verify beyond any doubt that someone was moving around Becky M. He took out a motion detector and pointed it at Becky M. Becky M. made no move and Scott carefully avoided the beam as he came near her with his EMF. Suddenly the motion detector went off. We were all looking at it and can verify that Scott did not break the beam of light. This seemed to frighten the child.

The little girl became uncomfortable with our equipment and us. At last she seemed to fade away.

Now Becky M. resumed her story. "Well Michael, he's four, used to have these horrible dreams. They were nightmares and he had them all of the time. He would wake up scared and sometimes crying. He kept insisting that there was a bad man in the room

Ecto mist in home of Becky M.   Photo by Becky Gummo

who was trying to start a fire. He would always point to the area where the chimney runs through his room. I've never seen anything, but most people who go onto the second floor feel like they are intruding on someone else's place.

"One night, while his dad was out, Michael and I were sitting in the living room watching television. It was an animal documentary but it was not funny or anything. Suddenly Michael began laughing. I glanced at him to see what was so funny and realized that he was watching the ceiling. I followed his eyes but saw nothing unusual.

"What are you laughing at," I asked him. "Don't you see the funny man, mom?' he asked. I told him that I didn't see anyone. Michael never looked away. He kept watching the ceiling. "Can't you see him, Mom? He's funny just flying around up there and waving. I think he likes making me laugh." For nearly 20 minutes Michael continued to watch the acrobatics of the secret show of the "laughing man" as Michael called him.

Now we knew of three entities in the building. There was the angry man on the second floor, the flying man on the first, and a little girl also on the first floor. Becky M. certainly had not exaggerated when she described the house as haunted.

Among the odd incidents that Becky M. had related to me was one that took on new meaning as we realized that one of the spirits is that of a little girl. During the Christmas season of 1999 Becky M. and her husband held a Christmas party at their home. During the evening a woman came up to Becky M. and asked her what was with the door in the kitchen. Becky M. looked at the door the woman indicated and smiled. It was the door to the upstairs and she thought she knew exactly what was going on. Every once in a while the door would open itself slightly and stay that way for a few seconds before closing again. Then the process would repeat itself. Becky M. knew that at the top of the stairs was the room that her two little children shared. Her son, Michael, was supposed to be sleeping, but obviously he wanted to watch the party instead.

Becky M. worked her way toward the door unobtrusively, intending to surprise the child and scold him for not being in bed. Suddenly Becky M. threw open the door expecting to see a startled little boy, instead no one was there. There was also no sound of scurrying feet or a glimpse of pajamas turning the corner of the stairs. Puzzled now, Becky M. went up the stairs quickly expecting to find her son playing possum. Instead she found a little boy sound asleep. The baby was also sleeping. Now she was really puzzled. Who had been peeking at the party? Now that we had confirmed the little girl ghost, Becky M. thought she understood that incident quite well.

The house actually had an interesting history. Originally the first floor was a small store for the community. The second floor would have been living quarters and behind the house was a smaller, older structure with a primitive fireplace dating the property back to the mid-1700's. This building, I feel sure, was the original homestead and the larger house was built later when the family prospered. This history would become important when we moved the investigation to the second floor.

The reason Becky M. had written to me in the first place was that her son was seeing a "bad man" in his room who frightened him terribly. He said that the man was trying to start a fire; trying to burn him up. Recently he had insisted that when he had looked under his parents' bed for a toy a "mask" had looked at him. He insisted that this was the face of the "bad man." Becky M. had actually grown so desperate to be believed about this that she had taped her conversation with Michael about the "mask" under the bed. He did insist that he saw a "mask" of the "bad man" who had floated out from under the bed and out the window toward the road. Perhaps it could have been written off as a daydream except that this child was truly frightened.

The incident that had actually precipitated the letter to me had been even more sad and desperate. One day Becky M. had put the children down for a nap then went outside for a few moments. She was only a few feet from the kitchen door and the children, but it was a few feet too far for Michael. When Becky M. came back inside, she heard a curious thud, thump sound. She went upstairs thinking that Michael was playing when he should be napping. At the top of the stairs she could only stop and stare in disbelief for a second. Michael had gotten an old, dull machete from somewhere and was chopping the wall at the chimneypiece where he insisted the "bad man" stayed.

Becky M. ran over and took the big knife away from her son. She started to scold him for damaging the wall, but then Michael started to tell her why. He said that the "bad man" was going to kill him-- that the bad man had said that, "I will die here." The child told his mother that he was trying to "kill the bad man." This child was very frightened.

Becky M. would later learn that the machete had belonged to her husband prior to her coming to live at the house. He had taken it down and stuffed it in a box that he had then tucked under the bed so that the children could not get it when Michael was born. That this child had been resourceful enough to get the machete and desperate enough to think he had to use it to defend himself spoke volumes about his emotional state.

Downstairs Becky Gummo had been fairly quiet and had not seemed to have much of an opinion about what was happening, but on the second floor this changed. Immediately she sensed something nasty. (I have been careful not to say evil for this was just the energy of a nasty, angry man, not of an evil entity which is very different.)

Scott began running his EMF meter and quickly picked up something in the bedroom/bathroom area. Immediately he located the outlets, lights, etc. to be sure that he was not picking up on those. This energy was in a column as tall as a man most of the time.

In Becky M.'s bedroom Al suddenly got that dizzy feeling that he has in the presence of a spirit. He grabbed at the wall and snapped a shot. Behind him Becky Gummo took a photo and in her picture there was what appears to be ectoplasm moving by Al.

Al and Scott worked as a team to locate the entity once more and found it in the bathroom. Here Scott traced it as it moved around the room and disappeared into a solid wall. This was exciting for this entity seemed to move unperturbed by present architecture. In his time, this was a single dwelling and he saw it that way still. He came and went at will.

We all left the second floor with an impression that this man was very angry with people being in his house. He wanted them out. He seemed to be just a nasty man who enjoyed frightening a little boy. Of course, there are those in the field of parapsychology who would say that he drew energy from the fright he gave that child.

Becky M. had told me prior to coming to the house that in the other side a religious family lived. She said that they were nice but did not believe in ghosts. Still, there had been odd incidents that led her to believe that they were experiencing the haunting, too.

One night Becky M. had gone out with the entire family to visit her mom who lives in Altoona. It grew late and her mother invited them to stay. As the children were already asleep, it seemed like a good idea and they accepted. The next day Becky M. had occasion to speak to the neighbor woman. The lady was cordial but she asked Becky M. what they had been doing in the attic in the middle of the night. Becky M. informed her that no one had been home so they could not have been in the attic. The neighbor knew that the only entrance to the attic was on Becky M's side of the house and she looked at her oddly. She told Becky M. that someone had to have been home and had been in the attic as they had been awakened by footsteps overhead in the wee hours of the night.

On another occasion Becky M. had known that the neighbors were away and she heard footsteps as if someone was walking on the second floor of that side of the house. This also occurred when that side of the house was not rented.

Becky M. mentioned that her feelings of the little girl on the first floor had decreased soon after the current neighbors had moved in. She speculated that this might have something to do with the fact that the neighbors had two little girls. Wouldn't a ghostly little girl feel attracted to the play of two other little girls?

Mist in workshop of Becky M.'s home   Photo by Becky M.

Becky M. had sent along some photographs of her house and the old house behind that was now used as a work shed by her husband. In one photo of the old house there was what appeared to be mist coming up through the floor and floating freely. I immediately asked Becky if anyone had been smoking or if there had been any smoke in the room for any other reason. "No," she said. "They had taken the photo of the table saw for insurance purposes, and no one had been smoking."

We all went out to the old house and I thought that it was lovely. It was a shame to see such a beautiful building turned into a tool shed, but that was neither here nor there. In the large, main room a huge, old fieldstone fireplace stood. I could well imagine a pioneer woman stirring a pot on that hob. A door led to a set of stairs and into the second level. As it was an area of storage that had become very cluttered, I allowed Al and Scott to climb up. Al immediately got that light-headed feeling again and snapped some photos with his digital camera. He got what appeared to be orbs looking out the window. This was odd, as someone else had confided to me earlier that he felt as if someone was watching us from that window. Becky Gummo had also said the same thing to Scott and Al.

After we left the old house we decided to visit the two small church cemeteries that border the backyard of this property. Becky M. had asked us if some of what they were experiencing could have come from there. I have heard of it happening before, but first I wanted to know if there was even any activity in those little cemeteries? I would be surprised by how much we found.

Al picked up on some energy and Becky shot a photo of him being followed by energy. At one point Scott called out that he was getting spikes on his

Cemetery behind Becky's house - Sept. 2000 Becky Gummo

EMF and again Becky took a picture. The results were amazing. Becky felt drawn to a new grave and snapped a shot of it with supercharged electrical energy above it. (That is shown on the cover photograph.) The area was very active. I would not be surprised if much of the haunting that Becky M. and her family has experienced is related to this cemetery.

By the time we left Becky M. that night she felt validated and less like she was alone in this situation. Experiencing a haunting can make you feel isolated. You don't know who will believe you and who will call you a nut. By the time folks feel desperate enough to contact someone, they are often cut off from traditional sources of support. Family members will deny it, clergy will suggest psychological help because they don't want to deal with it, and others will snigger and call them crazy. I know that Becky M. felt better, but we did counsel her to get Michael out of the house as it was affecting him so badly, or to at least take control and tell the "bad man" to stop scaring her son.

Postscript:

Becky M. did take control of the situation and told the entity to behave and leave her children alone. It seemed to help the situation until she left the house.

A HAUNTED HOUSE IN YOUNGWOOD

(Youngwood, Westmoreland County)

Early in the summer of 1999 my friend Becky Gummo invited me to ride along with her to visit a friend she met over the internet who's home was supposed to be haunted. She had also invited another friend she had made over the internet along. This gentleman and his wife, Al and Joanne Brindza would turn out to be great friends for both of us, but on that first day we were more interested in ghosts than anything else. We met at the home of a young couple in Youngwood named Melissa and Eric. They share their home with a good friend named Duane and their two little girls.

Melissa and Eric had come to rent their large old home in Youngwood, PA in February of 1998. It was a time of great change for them all, but especially for Melissa. Three months earlier the young couple had gotten married. Then she had only recently given birth to their first child, a baby girl. The pregnancy and birth were difficult for Melissa, and was made more so when it was discovered that she'd need a cesarean section delivery. A time of great joy became an anguishing wait for Melissa's family and Eric when they nearly lost both Melissa and the little baby. Melissa went to stay with her mother, a nurse, after being released from the hospital. She was in a lot of pain and could not do very much for herself or the baby at that point. It was up to Eric and Duane to get the couple's possessions moved into their new home. The men moved furniture, set up the nursery and tried to make the place habitable so that when Melissa arrived there would be little for her to do. They both understood that for a while Melissa was not going to be able to do much more than care for herself and the baby.

When Eric finally was able to go pick Melissa and the baby up from her parents' home, it must have been a great relief for him. The young couple was now able to begin their new life. Much had changed for them in three months; marriage, a baby and moving to a new town completed the changes. However, Eric must also have felt a great responsibility, as he knew that Melissa was still in a lot of pain and would need a lot of extra care.

If there was one thing that Melissa did not enjoy about her current situation, it was the pain and the strong medication that they had given her for it. Whenever she could, she'd find ways around taking the medicine. One thing that helped reduce her pain and left her without the sleepiness and lethargy that she hated was a soothing bath. Her first night in her new home Melissa put the baby down to sleep and decided to take a bath. While she relaxed in the tub, she gradually became aware of someone on the floor above her walking about and moving something heavy. Her first thought was, "Well, the neighbors upstairs are moving their furniture again." She had most recently lived in an apartment complex and was very familiar with that sound. As quickly as the thought came, a second one followed. This was a single-family house with an attic. Since they were still moving in and settling down it was not unreasonable that someone would be upstairs in the attic thumping and dragging stuff around, but who? She thought Eric was downstairs, so maybe Duane? Curiosity got the best of her and she called for Eric. She heard him running up the stairs from the first floor.

"Where's Duane?" She asked him as soon as he stepped into the bathroom.

"Down the street at his girlfriend's house," Eric said, "Why?"

Melissa tried to remain calm, but the knowledge that she had been hearing footsteps above her made her a bit unnerved. "Well who's in the attic?"

"No one," Eric answered, with a puzzled look. "Why?"

"Either we have giant squirrels or something because someone has been up there walking around and dragging something. I thought maybe Duane was dragging boxes around getting them arranged."

Eric listened but all he heard was silence. This was Melissa's first indication that they might be sharing their home with someone unseen, but it certainly would not be her last. However, Melissa was not one to jump to conclusions and she began to wonder if the stress of recent events had made her imagine the footsteps and dragging noise above her. She had also written off that feeling of being watched and a thick electric feeling "like right before a thunderstorm" as part of the stress and medication she was taking.

During the next several days Melissa settled in as best she could. Usually she tried to stay upstairs where the bed, baby supplies and bathroom were because navigating the stairs with her stitches was painful. Eric did most of the running for bottles and the like but one night, after they had been there two weeks, the baby awoke in the middle of the night and wanted a bottle. Eric was sleeping soundly, so Melissa decided that she'd hobble down and get the bottle so Eric could rest.

Melissa made a detour into the dining room where the kitchen light switch was located and reached to flip it. On the far side of the room sat a large plastic garbage can filled with curtain rods, blinds and other window treatments. It had sat there for the past two weeks as they had slowly been using the items as they had a chance. Suddenly the can tipped itself over and fell. It flew forward toward the doorway and would have made it into the entry hall if it hadn't struck the doorframe and rolled backward. Melissa stared at it for a moment in the semi-light of the streetlights coming in the windows. That can had moved as if someone had given it a hard shove. There was no reason why it should have fallen over. The can was sitting on the level floor, yet it had shot forward to roll rapidly across the floor. Melissa made a mental decision not to let this upset her. She got the bottle from the kitchen and hurried back upstairs as quickly as her stitches would allow.

Through the next few weeks there would be a series of little things that were just odd. A feeling that you were being watched. The flash of someone caught moving by when she was in bed reading. Just little things that left her with a feeling that there was someone else in the house--someone she could not quite see. There were footsteps in the hall, on the basement stairs and even out on the back porch. They heard someone walk up the stairs to the second floor, but whenever they looked no one was ever there.

The landlords were still working on some papering and painting in the house when the young couple had moved in. Melissa got to know the landlord's wife *Jill fairly well. Melissa's friend, *Leslie, who lived just down the street in another house owned by the same landlords, was getting to know Jill, too. One day Melissa decided to ask Jill if they might know if the house had a history of being haunted.

Melissa was, however; still reluctant to use the word "haunted." She only asked if Jill knew if anything "odd" had happened there. The reaction from Jill was surprising. Immediately she became very defensive. "I don't know what you're talking about. There's nothing wrong with this house--nothing at all!" With that Jill gathered up some supplies and immediately left.

Melissa went down to talk to her friend Leslie later that day and told her about the odd reaction Jill had to her question. "Oh, it's not as odd as you think," Leslie told her. "Jill came down here earlier to take care of some stuff and she started talking about what happened up at your house. She was really upset. She kept telling me not to tell you, but they already know that your house is haunted. They lived there once for a little while."

Melissa felt relieved. A ghost, as disconcerting as it might be for most folks, was preferable to feeling like she was imagining things. Now she felt validated in her observations. She had a lot of questions, but Leslie could not answer them yet. Jill had to know that by telling Leslie about the haunting Melissa would learn of it. She was well aware that Leslie and Melissa were good friends. The two friends thought it was perhaps Jill's way of confirming the haunting while she was maintaining her ability to deny it officially. Jill had said that she was afraid that if Melissa and Eric learned that the house was haunted they might move. Worse yet, from Jill's standpoint, she did not want the house to gain a reputation or else it might be impossible to rent it out.

One afternoon Melissa was laying in bed resting when she heard the baby cooing as she did when she was being talked to and played with. The crib was near the bed and Melissa opened her eyes to check on the baby. The baby lay there cooing and smiling and jiggling around but no one was there. The mobile, that was a wind up model, was moving as if someone had given it a sharp tap. It was unusual enough that Melissa noted it mentally while she watched. It had nothing to do with the baby's movements and the baby was much too small to reach up and bat it herself.

On another day Melissa came upstairs and peeked into the master bedroom where the crib was still set up. The baby, who was then about four months old, was laying on her side sound asleep. It was a position that Melissa knew well by now. She listened to her little girl breath for a few seconds before starting down the hallway quietly. Suddenly the little girl let out a terrible scream. Melissa responded immediately. This was not the normal sound of her baby awaking; it was a sound of fear. She whirled around and, as she stepped into her bedroom, a blast of cold air struck her. "I mean it felt like stepping into a meat locker" Melissa would later tell us. As the cold air slid past her, Melissa gathered up the baby who settled into little whimpers. Melissa knew that someone had passed her, but someone she certainly felt, but could not see.

Through time Melissa was able to piece together more of the history of the house. It was built around 1900 by an immigrant man who had bought the ground and built it for his family in the old country. This man had been a railroad worker and when he had built his home and saved enough money for passage, he had been able to send for his family. This made her think that this man certainly must have loved this place greatly. It meant a lot to him and she learned that he had lived in the house for the rest of his life. In fact, he had died of old age either in the living room or master bedroom of the house.

She also heard a story that would explain to her something that not only she had been feeling but many of their guests had felt as well. There was always a feeling of "anxiety" and of being watched from the porch. Several guests had felt as if someone was looking in the window at them and watching. This feeling of anger and of being watched was one Melissa knew well herself. Now she was beginning to understand it--that was if the story was true. To date she has never been able to verify it in the local newspapers.

According to the story she was told, in the 1940's a man crossing the busy highway that fronts the house was struck by a car. The man had apparently been carrying packages and had not seen the car coming. He had stepped down off the sidewalk directly into the path of a fast moving vehicle. The impact had thrown the poor man across the street onto the front porch of the house where he had died on impact. Since that time people had felt or sensed that the man's spirit was still there and angry or upset-perhaps even confused--about what had happened to him.

The family's experiences with this particular spirit would be quite overt. When Melissa was eight months pregnant with her second daughter, she was downstairs late one afternoon playing Nintendo while Eric was napping upstairs with their first little girl. Suddenly she heard thumping on the porch as if something had fallen. She leaned back on the couch and looked out the window, but no one was there. She went back to playing her game, but the sounds interrupted her again. This time the sound was more like some-one slamming something hard onto the floorboards of the porch. Wack! Wack! Wack! Someone was slamming something around on her porch!

Again Melissa leaned back to see what was going on. At that moment one of the three plastic chairs that had sat on the porch for nearly two years went flying by as if thrown hard. It struck the woodwork at the top of the porch and fell back with a thud.

Melissa struggled up and ran to the door. Who would have thrown the chair? She stepped out into the cold of the winter afternoon. She saw no one and no one was walk-ing down the street. She stepped around the turn of the wrap-around porch but no one was on the porch or going down that side of the house either. She picked up the chair and put it back in place. Melissa would have no easy explanation for this occurrence for it was a cold, clear and calm day with "virtually no wind at all."

Another night about three a.m. Melissa was working on the computer. Her younger sister was there and they were talking while she worked. Suddenly, the quiet of the night was interrupted by strong pounding on the front door. Melissa recognized the sound immediately for the door was old and the glass panes in it rattled when it was beaten upon. Her first thought was that Duane was out that night and must have returned to find he had forgotten his keys. She got up and, with her sister, started downstairs. The quality of the sound of knocking changed so that she thought Duane was now beating on the wall beside the door. Melissa flipped on the light and looked out, but no one was there. She thought that perhaps some drunk had accidentally stumbled onto the wrong porch, then realized his mistake.

She and her sister started back upstairs. When Melissa was nearly at the top of the steps, the pounding started again on the other side of the wall near the door. Melissa turned around to answer it thinking that she was going to give someone a few choice words. But when she got to the glass door, no one was there. She flipped the lock quick-ly and hurried onto the porch, but no one was there either. She quickly looked both ways down the sidewalks, but still no one could be seen. "I'm not coming downstairs again. Feel free to spend the night here if you want to," she said aloud as she turned and hurried back inside. That ended the pounding on the porch for that night.

Though Melissa has no proof that this entity is to blame, she suspects that he might be responsible for one of the most upsetting things that ever happened to her in the house. The first Christmas they spent there, Melissa put the Christmas tree in the dining room so that it would be out of the way of the baby who was just beginning to crawl. She also wanted to be able to put the antique glass ornaments her grandmother had given her on the tree. Right after she put it up in the room she came downstairs in the middle of the night to find the tree had somehow fallen or been pushed over. She picked it up and for-tunately there was little breakage of the decorations. She gathered them up and put them back on the tree after giving it a good shake and making sure that it was level and secure.

The next night she came down for the regular bottle in the middle of the night and found the tree had not only been tipped over again, this time it had been thrown about four feet away from where she had placed it. Whoever had thrown it had done so with suffi-cient force to break her antique ornaments. She tried to pick up the tree and clean up the mess, but the tree refused to stay up despite her best efforts. She could see no logical rea-son why it would not stand up, but it just kept falling over every time she'd get it placed upright. She was very upset about her grandmother's ornaments and complained about them while she cleaned up the shattered glass.

In the morning she asked Duane and Eric if they could get the tree put back up. She explained what had happened during the night and showed them where she had found it. The men quickly put the tree back up and this time it stayed put. It frustrated Melissa for she had done exactly the same thing during the night, only to have the tree tipped back over. She could not help feeling that someone was angry about where she had put the tree. From that day forward, though, the tree never tipped over again.

Throughout their tenure in the house, Melissa also found that a newborn baby seemed to haunt the house. Several times she has heard its cry and gotten up to answer it before realizing that it was not her baby. One day, however, she had an experience that convinced her once and for all that a baby haunted the house.

Melissa, the baby and Eric were at Leslie's house down the street. Duane was also out. Melissa and Leslie were talking about a certain book and Leslie asked if she could borrow it. Melissa said that it would be fine and got up to run back up to the house to get it before she forgot. She came in, grabbed the book, and turned to go when very clearly she heard the thin wail of a newborn crying. In her haste, she turned back without think-ing. Her motherly instincts were working and she started up the stairs thinking that her own baby must have awakened. Suddenly it struck her that her baby was down the street with Eric. She went up the steps and looked around anyhow. The sound seemed to be coming from a room that was then used for storage. When she got there, though, the sound simply stopped.

Perhaps the most dramatic haunting would be that of the shadows. Three different times she has seen a black column about eight feet high pass through her bedroom. One night her skeptical husband also witnessed the black column moving quickly through their bedroom. This always happened between 3 and 3:30 a.m. in the morning and Eric explained that he had tried to come up with a logical explanation for this. He had explored the possibility that it was something about car lights going pass the room. However, the lights looked totally different and always passed by from left to right. This column always moved by from right to left and passed by when no one was driving through. Melissa described it like this, "It's all dark shadow, not really humanoid, but that shape (a column) and it moved in one smooth movement."

Eric, for all of his skepticism, would have an experience that he would not be able to explain away. One day he was walking from the living room across the foyer to the kitchen which meant that he had to pass the stairs that lead to the second floor. As he did so, a quick movement caught his attention. He looked up in time to see a black shadow, clear, distinct and separate from the wall, making the turn up the stairs. This experience still puzzles him. He tried his best to explain what he saw and kept insisting that I under-stand that this was an image that stood out in space away from the wall. It was opaque enough that, though he could see through the black shadow, it would have been difficult to make out what was on the other side.

Many other events have occurred which have convinced them that the house certain-ly is haunted. As their oldest little girl grew up, she began offering bites of food and bot-tles to an invisible someone. She has now grown up enough to speak and from time to time she'll suddenly look out into the foyer, up the stairs or out into the hallway of the second floor and ask her mommy "Who's that?" Inevitably when Melissa looks, there is no one there.

The couple's second child has some developmental problems and one day Melissa left her on the floor with a favorite toy laying across the room. The little girl was not yet crawling and Melissa hoped that this would encourage her to try. Melissa stepped out of the room for just a second and turned around to find that, though the child had not moved, she now had the toy. How could that have happened? Melissa believes that the spirit that is elderly and whom she believes is the builder of the house likes the children especially well and watches over them.

Melissa once did some dog sitting for her family. The dog seemed very attached to her and followed her everywhere; however, one day when she went into the dining room the dog refused to follow. It sat in the foyer looking in and began to whine and bawl. She said that several other times the dog would go into the dining room but it would hide under the table and seemed to be watching someone intently.

With so many spirits you'd think she wouldn't notice one more unless it made a big noise but, in fact, not making a big noise is what got this last specter noticed. From the very beginning Melissa would often hear someone talking while she was the lone adult in the house. For a long time she drove herself crazy trying to locate the clock radio, television or other electronic appliance that was making noise. She described what she heard as a man talking softly, but she could never locate the source of the sound, nor could she tell exactly what he was saying. No matter where she went in the house, the sound seemed to be somewhere nearby.

Duane, too, has heard this ghost talking and has looked for a radio or something to turn off. He never found anything turned on that could explain the sound. Now the family no longer responds to the talking ghost. Who he is or what he wants remains a mystery, but Melissa has heard him often enough that she no longer is concerned when he begins to talk softly.

Melissa did finally learn why Jill was so upset about her innocent question not long after she had moved in. Jill and her husband had inherited the house and had lived in it briefly. They had experienced the haunting as well. Something about the ghosts had frightened the family so badly that one night they had left in the middle of the night and never returned. The family stayed in hotels until they had another place to live.

Perhaps the haunting was different for Jill and her husband, or perhaps the fact of the haunting was just more than they could handle because it clashed with their belief system. However, Melissa, Eric, their children and friends have not only come to terms with the spirits in their home, they have made them part of the family. Melissa put it best when she said, "I've felt watched, I've heard things, seen things and felt things, but I've never been really frightened here. I have never had anything happen here that would make me want to move. None of the ghosts are frightening here except maybe the one on the porch. He's angry, he's pissed, no he has angst, but then I'd be pissed to if I tried to cross the street and wound up dead." Perhaps it is that attitude that keeps the haunting from becoming more pronounced.

Melissa and her family consider the house in Youngwood, ghosts and all, to be home and don't plan to move any time soon. Their acceptance is a large part of the reason why the ghosts are so benign. Melissa seems to look upon the ghosts as co-tenants, and she respects them as long as they let her family alone.

THE GHOSTLY CAST OF THE PITTSBURGH PLAYHOUSE

(Pittsburgh, Allegheny County)

Theaters have long been associated with ghostly phenomena and the skeptics among us would say that it is because actors are more imaginative than most, but I don't agree. In my opinion, it is because actors are more passionate than most. They live their entire lives hoping to please an audience. They express their hearts before hundreds of people each night and pour their emotions into a part. For many actors the theater, the pursuit of their craft, becomes a consuming passion, and that is why I believe so many actors and actresses stay behind after death. They return to the place where they felt loved and where they were able to touch other people with deep emotion.

The Pittsburgh Playhouse was not always the palace of dreams that it is today. Through the years there have been many incarnations. The Rockwell Theater was a Jewish synagogue. There was a bar in the lobby--though it no longer serves drinks--and a restaurant in the basement that has since become a storage area. The Theater Upstairs once housed a brothel, and there is an area behind the defunct bar that is called the catacombs. What today are dressing rooms was once part of a group of row houses. The energy in this place is diverse and lively.

The most well known spirit is that of famous Pittsburgh actor John Johns. He performed in the playhouse between 1950 and 1960. He found a great response from the people of Pittsburgh who hailed his ability. He loved his theatric home and knew nearly every inch of the place. One night in the basement restaurant, he suddenly fell to the floor with a massive heart attack. The stricken man was carried to Dressing Room 7 while they awaited help. Here Johns died just as they entered the room. The men who carried him in, laid a corpse upon the couch. Since that time, people have reported hearing footsteps hurrying to Dressing Room 7 where they instantly stop at the threshold.

Johns has been seen, too. A student group saw a man in a tuxedo looking over the props and scenery in the Hamlet Street Theater, which was very active during Johns' day. When they reported this odd fellow to the director, he could not find the man. He then questioned the students further and realized that their descriptions tallied with that of Johns. Others have reported seeing Johns sitting alone in the closed theater late at night after the last happy theatergoer has gone. People realize that this is Johns because his photograph hangs in the Hamlet Street Theater where he so often performed.

The ghost known as Weeping Eleanor has never been seen, but many folks have reported hearing a woman crying in the dressing rooms late at night. When they have explored to see who this sad woman is, there is never anyone there.

The story of this young woman is truly tragic. Long before this area was turned into dressing rooms for the theater, the row houses caught fire. As the fire quickly spread, everyone began to panic. Fire in a line of row houses could mean sure death. The alarm went out quickly and all of the houses were emptied, all except the house where today the dressing room stands. In that space a woman named Eleanor and her little daughter were trapped and they burned to death. Late at night Eleanor cries for the loss of her child and herself in such a horrible manner so long ago.

A male student wandered into the Hamlet Street Theater one afternoon during a rehearsal break. He was seeking solitude and sat in the dark, empty theater. Suddenly a woman in a white dress and a man in a black suit danced onto the stage as if in time to music he could not hear. The startled young man stared at the ghostly duo who promptly vanished. Apparently, some of the acts at the Hamlet Street are still running old shows!

A Lady in White has been reported in the Hamlet Street as well. This woman sachets across the balcony. She has also reputedly been seen in the Theater Upstairs where a brothel used to be. Today the Upstairs Theater is closed to the public and the area is now used for storage.

The stories of the Lady in White caught the attention of *Pittsburgh Press Family Magazine* in Oct. of 1978. They reported that a technical director for the playhouse known as "The Swede" had a very personal confrontation with the Lady in White.

Eight years earlier, "The Swede" had been in the building working upon the light fixtures when a woman in a white dress stepped on stage. The woman walked directly up to "The Swede" and raised a gun to point it at him. Then she simply disappeared. "The Swede" lost his reputation for being fearless and skeptical of ghosts. He quit work that very day and told them all exactly why!

Others have seen this same woman walking across the stage with her gun. However, she has not been known to point it at anyone else. Perhaps it was a good thing that "The Swede" did not stay around to find out what this might mean for him.

If ghosts wielding guns is not enough, there is also the hideous spirit of a green man known locally as "Gorgeous George, who haunts the theaters. His ghastly greenness is made even more horrible by the fact that his face is rotted. He has been seen behind the scenes of the theater knocking on the costume shop window until an actress looked up. He smiled and faded away. Others have reported seeing him near the props department.

Yet another spirit is associated with the most prolific and sensational of the hauntings. This character performs in the Rockwell Theater that had once been a synagogue. His first known appearance was in 1974 when a group of college students held a seance on that stage at midnight on Halloween. The students were expecting ghostly communications, but they got more than they had bargained for.

The students had been locked into the building and the telephone system had been shut off as usual. They had set up upon the stage. As midnight neared, they began the seance with candles lit and only the Ghost Light up to give the auditorium a subdued light. To their surprise, they did not receive any message from the dead, but one of them caught a glimpse of something moving in the back of the theater. They all stared into the shadows and there was a figure in red who was walking back and forth in a most agitated manner. As the young people watched him, they could see the man's face growing clearer and he wore a troubled expression. The man seemed to move more rapidly as he went until he suddenly levitated off of the floor and began bouncing into the walls. At one point he even bounced so hard that he touched the ceiling. It would have been enough to frighten most people, but they held their ground. After all, they had come to see a ghost.

An article in the *Pittsburgh Post-Gazette* from 1982 described the event from that point on. "...every phone in the place began to ring."

At this point, the lone female in the group grew very frightened. Her four companions turned to see what she was staring at and to their amazement there was an entire auditorium full of ghostly watchers in every seat--and they all wore clothing from around 1900!

That was enough for the students. They hurriedly left the building only to return the next morning to confide their story to the management.

Since that night, others have encountered the man in red. He's dressed as a Bouncing Red Meanie, (also known as Bouncing Loony) a clown character popular at the turn of the century.

But the ghosts are not all performers at the theater. What would a theater be without the ticket taker who quietly ushers all those happy, anticipating people into the realm of magic? The ticket office has it's own specter who, though not seen, is very much a presence. This spirit has rattled garbage can lids in the room, moved things about and played little pranks when the office is closed. Among the pranks are filing cabinets where all the drawers were pulled open in the locked office, a money box that would unlock and open itself, and banging sounds as if someone was slamming things around in the closed and locked room.

Of course, a skeptic would still be able to explain away the haunting reports, but for those who have seen, heard or felt the spirits of the Pittsburgh Playhouse no amount of rational explanation will sway them from their stories. Even some skeptics have told me that when they are alone in the building they don't look too closely into the shadows for fear they might see something they do not believe in.

DINGLE'S GHOST

(Roaring Spring, Blair County)

Folklore can be defined as oral or written stories passed down from generation to generation that have at least a kernel of truth in them. Legends also usually hold a kernel of truth as well. I was surprised one evening at a lecture in Blair County to hear some of the older folks asking me if I had ever heard of Dingle's Ghost? I had not and it surprised me because I thought that I had combed the historical archives of Blair County for almost every ghost story recorded. However, I had missed poor Dingle. The people who told me the story referred me to the Morrison Cove Herald Archives for proof that Dingle had existed and had died as they said he had. I'm going to pass on the story as it was told to me. I cannot say it is "true," but the one woman in particular said, "I know this story is true. I remember my mother and father saying about it. It was big talk back then." Here is Dingle's story and you can decide if you'd like to believe it or not.

According to the people I have spoken to, there was a local fellow early in the 1900's who used to haul wood and saw dust from a mill just outside of Roaring Spring back into town. He lived over near the spring for which the town has long been famous. The fellow was quite thrifty and industrious. In fact, someone unkind would have been able to call him miserly. He did not believe in banks, so he buried his money in mason jars around his property.

This fellow was out at the mill one day loading up when there was an accident. The accounts do not specify how it happened, but old Dingle fell and stumbled into the path of the saw. He was literally cut in half. (Others insisted that he had just his head cut off.)

The workers were justifiably horrified by the events and it took them a bit to recover sufficiently to gather up Dingle's two halves and load them onto the bed of Dingle's own wagon. He was conveyed back to town to the undertaker's establishment in his own wagon.

The owner of the sawmill was upset about the event, but business is business and he did not allow the mill to be shut down for long. In fact, it was reported that that as the accident had occurred in the morning, by noon the mill was running again.

In Roaring Spring, gossip had it that the there were bits of old Dingle that the saw had chewed up and strewn around still laying in the saw dust pile and the bushes beyond. However, two local men who went for sawdust that day did not report seeing the grisly sight.

A few evenings after Dingle was buried in the old cemetery up behind the mill people were startled when they heard a wagon and team rattling along the road from the mill into town. When the wagon hove into sight, there sat old Dingle's headless body at the reins. The wagon and horses turned into Dingle's property. Dingle jumped down off the wagon and hurried around the house into the back of his property where his money was supposedly buried in mason jars.

This certainly made a bit of a stir in town. Rumors of the ghostly ride of Dingle soon spread. Those who had seen him were adamant that his headless specter had come back to check on his money. Others, however, scoffed.

However, Dingle made another appearance a few nights later. His headless ghost came riding into town and down to his house near the spring. Once more he jumped down and hurried behind the house. Many times Dingle was to make this ride, and the woman who told me the most about the story insisted that her own parents had seen Dingle on his ghostly ride. She believed that story about as much as any ghost story she had ever heard because her folks weren't ones to exaggerate or lie.

As proof that the story is true, a local man brought in a copy of Vol. 11 of *Bygone Days In the Cove* by Ella M. Snowberger. He indicated a short item in the volume and said, "Now she doesn't mention anything about the ghost, but this is the report on Dingle's death and it even gives his real name. Dingle was a nickname, as I understood it."
This is exactly what the article read:

> **"Met Violent Death**
> Among Mr. Ferry's friends and acquaintances who met violent death were Billy Dick, who was sawed in two at a saw mill. Edward went with brother Frank shortly thereafter to get a load of sawdust. The two boys looked intently among the adjacent trees and shrubbery for bits of the torn flesh, which they had been told had been splattered about, but they could find none..."

Now this tiny tidbit in the remembrances of a local man certainly cannot verify the ghostly wanderings of Dingle, but at least like most folklore and legends it lends a bit of actual history to the story. As to whether you believe that Dingle's specter did return to check on his buried money or not, well that's a matter for those who witnessed his return to argue with those who will eternally be skeptical.

RETURN TO THE HAUNTED JEAN BONNET TAVERN

(Bedford, Bedford County)

Telling ghost stories is not like telling any other type of story. Traditionally a story must have a beginning, middle and ending. However, with a ghost story I sometimes don't have an ending. Many of the places that I write about are actively haunted, so I can only tell the story up until the time that the book is printed. The Jean Bonnet Tavern and Bed and Breakfast in Bedford County is just such a story. Furthermore, from time to time old items are unearthed that can change or clarify a story and this has happened at the Jean Bonnet.

The building site where the Jean Bonnet stands was part of the Seneca and Shawnee tribes' land holdings as treatied for with the Iroquois Nation. However, whites did not recognize Native land rights, so it became land up for grabs, and it did not take long before the land was grabbed up. The property, with a structure already existing, was in place in 1758 when the land became part of a William Penn Land Grant to Hance Ireland who purchased 690 acres on July 23, 1762. Hance ran the Hance Ireland and Company Land Speculation Firm in Cumberland County. By then an event had happened at the spot that would give rise to a ghost story.

During the fall of 1758 General Forbes moved from his post westward in hopes of taking Fort Duquesne from the French. Forbes began his march, but he stopped to wait for reinforcements to catch up with him. He found that he had to tarry five miles west of Raystown (Bedford) at what would become known as Plantation Farm, Twin Forks, and later the Jean Bonnet. While waiting here a few days, Forbes noticed that a particular teamster or trader was showing great interest in troop movement. He suspected that the man was a French loyalist or spy. This was not a bad assumption as there were many French in the area at that time. He feared that if word of a spy would reach the ears of his men they might desert, so he resolved the situation by trusting a few aides to apprehend the teamster quietly.

Local legend has always insisted that the man was tried and found guilty of spying. At this time the penalty for spying was instant death. However, Forbes did not want to risk loosing men who feared that the spy had gotten word through before being caught, so he tried and executed the man in secret. The body was said to have then been disposed of by burying it under the floor of the stone fort or building.

Much of the story cannot be substantiated, however there are parts that we know to be true. General Forbes was definitely at Raystown in the fall of 1758. He did leave Raystown to attack and claim Fort Duquesne for the British and he did cut the roads that would split and give the Jean Bonnet the name Twin Forks. Therefore, General John Forbes certainly was in the proper area at the right time. He did attack and take Fort Duquesne in November of 1758 along with among others Generals Washington and Col. Bouquet.

Furthermore, in Jones' *History of the Juniata Valley*, he dates the settlement of Raystown as beginning in 1751 when a man named Ray built three cabins near present-day Bedford. Ray was an Indian trader and Jones wrote, "In 1755 the province agreed to open a wagon road from Fort Loudon, in Cumberland County, (present day Fulton County) to the forks of the Youghiogheny River. For this purpose three hundred men were sent up, but for some cause or the other the project was abandoned." This would indicate that there were other settlers in the area at that time and give validity to the notion that though the official date of building for the tavern is 1764; a "fort" or stone structure that is now the basement or dining room predates that time.

Moving with men, provisions, and equipment, Forbes would probably not make more than five miles a day, particularly as he had to cut the road as he went in many areas or widen existing Native American trails. There is reason to suppose then; that General John Forbes might have taken up lodgings at the "fort" which is now the Jean Bonnet when he was in the area. He was moving his men and equipment in October and weather, troop reinforcements, or time needed to cut a larger, better road could have stalled Forbes in that area for days.

But the best proof that a spy was executed and buried beneath the floor of the fort, and that the fort would later become the nexus of the Jean Bonnet, lies in the fact that in 1957 the then owners of the tavern dug up the floor of the basement prior to having it cemented and found a long dead body buried there. The skeleton was determined to be male, and from the buckles and buttons it was believed to pre-date the Revolution. Perhaps this legend is true, after all.

For many years people have claimed to see a man who sits quietly at one of the tables and never speaks. They say he wears colonial garb. Others insist that footsteps, cold drafts and even a mist are manifestations of the spirit.

By the time this event supposedly occurred the fort had been in existence for at least forty years and had been abandoned by the French as the British pushed forward into the then French owned frontier. The original basement structure of the Jean Bonnet that is now the dining area could, therefore, predate the rest of the structure by at least forty years. There is little to prove the actual date of the building, but it had served as a French fort (unofficially) and was a trading post. The building was referred to as being on the way to the Old Shawnese Cabins--present day Shawnee State Park-- in trapper and trader accounts for many years before Forbes supposedly stopped over there. Furthermore, an inspection of the building itself does reveal a few tantalizing clues. The restaurant area has a large fireplace that is not in line with the fireplace on the tavern level. Usually a person building such a structure would use one central flue and chimney, as it required a great deal of work to build such a structure. This is not the case at the Jean Bonnet. We know that the

Mist on empty floor   Photo by Al Brindza

building was built for resale by a land speculator so it is unlikely that he'd foot the expense of two separate chimneys when one was the standard of the day. Furthermore, the mortaring is in a different style on the restaurant level fireplace than in the tavern level fireplace. This would indicate that two separate groups built the fireplaces at different times. Surely if a single group of men built the building they would have used the same mortaring style on both fireplaces.

Ireland commissioned to have the building now called the Jean Bonnet Tavern and Bed and Breakfast built, but at that time the porches were not on it. The building has gone through several significant changes or renovations through the years.

Ireland soon put the land up for sale and it was bought by Robert Callender and his wife Francis of Middle Township in Cumberland County. At this time the tavern and inn was called Plantation Farm. However, the name was a bit of a misnomer for Robert Callender did not farm it. He was an Indian trader.

Callender would one day become a scout for General Washington and it would always be said that he kept his mistress at Plantation Farm. During the Revolutionary War she was rumored to have worked at the tavern and she would run to the front of the building as she watched for Callender's return. She died while awaiting Callender who had promised to marry her after the war. Now there are some discrepancies in this story. Court House records indicate that Callender was married to a woman named Francis of Middle Township in Cumberland County. Either this Francis was the mistress; or else Francis never left Cumberland County and was unaware of her husband's liaisons. If so, either Robert Callender was lying to this unfortunate young woman, or else he was about to engage in bigamy.

What is known of Robert Callender is that he was quite a wealthy man, he enjoyed adventure and, as an Indian trader, conducted business with the Iroquois nation throughout Pennsylvania and New York. It is also known that he had several businesses. It would not be that difficult to imagine this adventuresome man enjoying both mistresses and Native women. Men of wealth and power in that time period often took both when the opportunity presented itself discretely, and it would not be likely that word from the then frontier would leak back to his respectable wife in their home.

Throughout the years many people have insisted that the spirit of a woman inhabits the hallway and bar of the tavern. In old newspaper accounts, the haunting is attributed

to the unfortunate mistress who was duped but did not know it. It is said that the rustle of crinoline skirts and the light footfalls of a woman are those of the mistress who is yet awaiting Callender's return so that she might still become his wife. If so, then this is truly a very sad haunting.

Jean Bonnet Photo from the Bedford Gazette Archive Provided by Melissa Jacobs

Callender and his wife eventually sold the tavern that was still called Plantation Farm to William and Isabell Neill of Baltimore Maryland. The Neill's took possession of the property in 1773, but as Neill was a land speculator he did not live at the Plantation Farm. Instead, he made money by reselling parcels of the original farm to the pioneers who were rushing into the area aided by the cutting of the military road from Carlisle to Fort Pitt. He also made money on quit rents and Plantation Farm was cut down from its original Penn Land Grant of 690 acres. At this time the tavern was pressed into service as a gathering place where white settlers could fight off the Seneca and Shawnee who were rightly upset that their land claims were being ignored and their homes destroyed

It was most probably during this time period that one of the most famous ghosts to haunt the property met his demise. On the first of each month, a local tavern was used as a meeting place for local court business. At that time, usually a well-to-do businessman or farmer would serve as judge and other local folks served as jury as local government business was brought up. At this time, Plantation Farm was being utilized both as a monthly courthouse and as a fort for locals against Indian attack. During a time when the local folks were gathered at the tavern for protection, such a court was held. At this time, a white man ran into the building begging protection from pursuing Shawnees. The last thing that the local folks wanted was trouble with the Shawnee who already were antagonized by the land grab. It was soon ascertained that this man was from Carlisle and had been in the area "trading" for horses. This was a euphemism for cheating the Natives out of horses.

Among the assemblage was a fellow who had recently arrived in the frontier from Carlisle. He recognized this man as a horse thief who was wanted in Carlisle, too. On the strength of this man's testimony, and probably because they hoped to appease the Shawnee with the dead body of the thief, a trial was held. The man was found guilty and quickly hung from the second floor staircase so that the body was suspended over the old, original staircase that is now a closed in closet. The body was then shown to the Shawnee before it was buried.

Through the years many folks have claimed to hear the heavy footsteps of a man walking the second floor hallway and down the original stairs. A cold breeze sometimes accompanies this spirit. This is believed to be the spirit of the horse thief. But if the horse thief does inhabit the second floor, he is usually said to be a nice fellow. However, Scott Crownover, who would later join the Central Pennsylvania Paranormal Association, told me that when he was investigating the haunting in the building he took his electromagnetic field detector (EMF) and his temperature probe into that area where the large walk-in cupboard or closet is and while holding them something sliced his thumb slightly. He believed that this was the displeased spirit of the horse thief who was upset at him for invading his space. Now Scott did not come to this supposition lightly, he did first look for any reasonable explanation, but could find none. He had touched nothing inside the closet and the equipment he carried was made of smooth plastic with rounded edges.

For many years, in fact until the late 1950's, an effigy of the lone horse thief hung from the second floor stairs up to the third level in remembrance of the thief's death long ago. Many people have claimed to hear his ghostly footfalls in the halls of the tavern and second floor.

Throughout the history of the tavern unknown numbers of men were tried, found guilty and executed by hanging outside or inside the building. Another group of six horse thieves were always said to have been hung outside the building. The proof of this event came when in the late 1800's a man plowing a field that adjoins the tavern grounds dug up six skeletons who had broken necks.

The tavern was purchased by John Bonnet, (Jean Bonnet) a French immigrant who changed the name of the business to *John Bonnet's Tavern*. John ran the tavern for several years before he died. His will specified that the tavern would go in equal shares to his son Isaac in Knox County, Ohio and his daughter Elizabeth. Isaac chose to sell his share to John Sill. Elizabeth kept her share and when she married John Ewalt he took over as innkeeper. John Sill also helped run the business.

In turn, John Sill would sell out to Simon Stuckey III and apparently Elizabeth and John Ewalt sold their shares, too, for there is no further mention of them in the records. Simon Stuckey III and his wife Margaret were Virginians who had moved to Pennsylvania years earlier and they purchased the tavern stand as an investment with an eye to its potential to help their 11 sons and six daughters get a start in life. Stuckey purchased some surrounding properties, too so that his land holdings around the tavern stand would total over 1000 acres.

It is unclear whether Simon Stuckey III ever lived in the tavern as he hired John Sill, the former owner, to run the business for him. At this time, Simon Stuckey III wanted to disassociate the tavern from the Bonnet family, so he chose to rename it. It became the *Forks Tavern* in reference to its position at the junction of two roads.

Simon Stuckey III would suffer the all too common tragedy, at that time, when his wife Margaret died. He would remarry to a widow named Eve Phillips who brought with her two small children from her first marriage. Not long after the couple was married, one of Eve's little children died and shortly thereafter, so did Simon Stuckey.

In his will, Simon left the property to his son David Stooky (David had changed the spelling of his name). David ran the Inn for a time before his brother George took over. Through time, each of the children took pieces of the property and sold or built on them. George would incur numerous debts while running the tavern and further property would be sold off to cover his debts. By the time the Stuckey family sold the property, there were only 85 acres left.

The property would be purchased in the mid-1800s by the Sauser family who would use the building as a private residence. It would be while the Sauser family owned the property that a field near the tavern was dug up. Unearthed were six skeletons with broken necks. The men had been buried in a row. Were these the six horse thieves in the gang that legend says were hung at the building? Most probably these were the horse thieves, but at the very least these skeletons were more proof of the tavern's period as a monthly courthouse.

The property would pass into the hands of the Enyearts in 1957. The Enyearts would own the property for 28 years. It was during this period that the name of the tavern once more became the Jean Bonnet Tavern and Bed and Breakfast. The Enyearts would be the ones to discover the lone skeleton underneath the floor of the basement (restaurant) area while working on renovations. In fact, the Enyearts would restore much of the building through their many years.

It would be during their tenancy that the stories of the many hauntings at the Jean Bonnet would begin to reach the public. Mrs. Enyeart was quite open about the many haunting experiences at the building. Of course, skeptics might point out that the ghosts were only the imagination of a creative woman, however, others were also experiencing the ghosts. In fact, in 1976 Bedford Gazette reporter, Mary Anna Mikula would do a story about the ghosts at the Jean Bonnet and she would report a very interesting tale.

Near the end of the 1960's, Westinghouse Electric Corp. was engaged in building a plant near the tavern. A young engineer working on the project took up residence at the Jean Bonnet. One night, the young man seemed slightly distressed and when questioned, he informed the Enyearts that he had just felt someone brush past him on the stairs in the lower hall. He had heard the rustle of

Scott Crownover Photo provided by Scott Crownover

33

crisp cloth and felt the person, but he saw no one.

Through the years, many other incidents have been reported. From sightings of a young boy lugging a heavy coal shuttle on the basement level to phantom footsteps of a woman who is heard but not seen, the stories have become legion. Numerous people have claimed to see a man sitting at one of the tables in the inner dining room, but when they look back the fellow is gone. Upstairs, people have complained about someone touching them at the bar, but no one is nearby.

Perhaps one of the most dramatic sightings occurred to a female bartender and her male friend years before Shannon and Melissa Jacobs, the present owners, had purchased the building.

One night, the bartender was working when a friend of hers came in. Through the course of the evening, the fellow had too much to drink. When it was time to close up, she and her male companion were afraid to let the inebriated fellow drive. As the guy lived nearby, they decided to lock up, take the man home, and then return to finish cleaning up. The woman had the keys and knew that this would be fine with the owners.

They took the man home and returned to the tavern. As they walked along the porch, they glanced in the window of the bar. Sitting there was a solitary man who was sipping a drink. That was impossible for they had made sure the bar was empty before leaving.

Still, the fellow had gotten in somehow. Quickly they unlocked the door and hurried into the bar. No one was there, but the building is big, so did the man hear them coming and hide? The two immediately ruled out anyone hiding in the upper levels because they had the key that unlocked the iron grillwork that separated the bar from those floors. However, someone could have gone down the stairs to the restaurant. They mounted a search but found no one. This upset the woman so much that after duly reporting the events to the then owners; she did not often mention the story. After that night, she also refused to be the last person to leave the building. She was afraid that the fellow might return for another drink.

But employees are not the only ones to experience the hauntings. Guests have reported many encounters as well. Scott Crownover decided to spend a night at the tavern to see if he would have an encounter. He invited a group of friends and a few members of the Central Pennsylvania Paranormal Association along. The group would not be disappointed. They rented the attic apartment that was then for let and went down to dinner. Afterwards, they went up to the bar where one of the men felt someone touch him. While they were discussing that, a woman heard them and came over. She said that the conversation had caught her ear as she had just experienced being touched by someone at the edge of the bar a little earlier. She, too, insisted that no one was near her.

The group would experience a few other oddities including the fact that they caught some orbs in the attic of the building. But the most unusual occurrence to come from that night would also take place in the bar. Al Brindza, who would not describe himself as sensitive (but he is), was in the bar watching the activity. Now Al is a confirmed non-drinker, so he felt a bit out of place in the bar. However, he tried to concentrate upon his feelings, despite the loud voices and the piano playing at the other end of the room. Suddenly he glanced at the one doorway that led into the hallway. Looking through the door were a group of people in rough clothes. Al called them "frontier type" clothes. The group was watching the man playing piano at the other end of the room. Al described his experience as "like trying to watch two televisions at once." He was aware of the real people at the bar, but he was equally drawn by those looking in from another time. This lasted a few seconds, but when he looked away and back again, they were gone.

Upstairs in the apartment the group began running their ghost hunting equipment and Scott picked up a couple odd readings. However, it was not until he tried to peek into the cubbyhole in the ceiling of the master bedroom in the attic that they experienced real activity. Suddenly the little Mag light he was using went out. Now Scott immediately told Al about it and Al snapped a series of photographs in which there were orbs.

Scott got down and looked at his flashlight. The bulb had burned out. He tried to unscrew the cap at the back of the light to get out the extra bulb there, but could not. In the next few minutes, Scott would realize how unusual this experience really was. He could not get the cap off the back of the flashlight despite the fact that he had taken the cap off earlier to put new batteries in. Eventually, he found out that the threads of the cap had been literally stripped, but by what?

Jean Bonnet vortex by Scott Crownover

The group wandered around the building for a good part of the night. At one point, they found themselves in the private dining room called the Forbes Room on the second level just across the hall from the bar. By now, some of Scott's guests were feeling a bit frustrated because nothing had happened to them. One female friend sat down in the little private dining room and said, "Well, if there's something here I wish it would show itself!"

Immediately Al and Scott scolded the young woman. One of the protocols of the Central Pennsylvania Paranormal Association is that we do not use ouija boards, participate in seances nor do we invite activity. We wish to chronicle whatever activity already exists, but we certainly don't want to stir up something that could adversely effect other folks.

While Scott was explaining this to the young woman, Al suddenly started to feel dizzy. Something was in the room with them and he could feel it. At just about the same time Al's camera, which was setting on the table, flashed as if someone had clicked it. No one had touched the camera--at least no one living.

Al felt that this entity was a female and that she often inhabited that room. Later, Kelly Weaver, would visit the Jean Bonnet and among the observations she made, was one I found very interesting. She walked into the same room and said, "I get a lot of female energy in here. It is as if there are some females here all the time. One seems to keep looking out of the window for someone." I could not help but marvel at Kelly's insights. Of course, one of the ghosts is to be the young bar maid who was looking for the return of her lover. However, very few folks knew the second tidbit of information that I was about to confide to Kelly. This same room was the ladies' room where women would sit to enjoy refreshments because they were not welcomed in the bar. That was strictly male territory and off limits to "nice" women.

By the time Scott and his guests left the Jean Bonnet the next morning, most of them were convinced that the Jean Bonnet indeed was haunted.

One of the most recent incidents took place in late November of 2000. A beer distributor from Altoona, named Bob, who services the bar decided to bring his twelve-year-old son and a friend to the Jean Bonnet for the Sunday night before Buck Season. This would be the boy's first hunting season and his father wanted to do something special to make it memorable.

The group got to the area early in the day, but they spent it visiting and tramping through the woods. By eight p.m., the trio was quite tired. They tramped into the inn and went to their room. The men and boy soon fell asleep, but about ten p.m. Bob awoke feeling terribly hot. Though the room had been quite pleasant when they had fallen asleep, now it was oppressively hot. His mouth felt dry and he needed a drink. He could clearly hear the sounds of the bar below them. There were glasses clanking, people laughing and a jazzy sort of music playing. He thought it sounded like something from an old jukebox. Bob pulled on his jeans and shirt. His son and friend woke up and he told them that he was going down to the bar for a glass of juice and to ask the bartender to turn down the heat in their room. His son and friend nodded because they were hot, too.

Bob did not even bother putting on his shoes before he padded down the stairs to the bar. He still heard the sounds people talking, laughter, glasses and that Jazzy music. However, his way into the bar was blocked by a black iron gate. Bob stared through the grates in shock. The bar was dark, quiet and obviously closed. Still the sounds had been so real that Bob found himself hurrying back up the stairs to look out the window to see if there were other cars in the parking lot. There were no cars besides his own.

Bob went back to his room and asked his son and his friend if they had heard the bar sounds. They all agreed that they had heard the same sounds that Bob had. The next day, Bob would tell his story to Melissa Jacobs. Melissa informed him that on Sunday nights the bar closes at 9 p.m., an hour before he awoke and heard those sounds. She would later check with the bartender who assured her that he did close on time. Furthermore, I have to tell you that I personally found that fact that Bob's room was oppressively hot unusual. Anyone who has ever spent a night in an old stone house in the middle of winter will tell you, that the bedrooms are hard to heat. The bedrooms at the Jean Bonnet are no different than any other bedroom in an old stone house. They do have heat in each room, but it usually only keeps them comfortable and certainly not HOT!

The fact that the room was oppressively hot becomes more significant when you know that temperature changes are nearly always associated with ghostly phenomena. Usually, people talk about a chill, a sudden coldness, however, the opposite, though more unusual, can also be true. Some hauntings are associated with heat rising.

Two nights later another couple was staying in the inn. The couple were the only guests that night. The next morning at breakfast Melissa asked them how the night had been. The couple responded pleasantly enough, however, they were curious as to who came in at 4 a.m. and why an employee needed to come in that early since breakfast was not served until after 8 a.m. Melissa assured them that she was usually the first person in the building in the morning and that she usually did not arrive until around 7 a.m. The couple looked at her oddly. They both insisted that they clearly heard someone come up the steps to the inn door, unlock the door, and come inside. They heard the person walking around the bar area below them and the hallway. The noise had actually awakened them both. Melissa could not explain what they had experienced. She only knew that she had been the first person in that morning and the doors had been locked as usual.

Of course, Melissa has had her own experiences in the building. Soon after purchasing it, she began to notice that every time she went past the door to the then unrented attic apartment the door would be in a different position. If it was closed when she first passed it, then it would be wide open a few minutes later when she came by again. One morning, she noticed this occurring several times and she decided that someone had gotten into the building somehow and was playing a trick on her.

Melissa went to her office on the tavern level to await a salesman who was coming in. When the man arrived, Melissa explained the situation to him and asked if he'd accompany her on a search of the building. He agreed. The two went past the apartment door that was open as they began searching the bedroom level. A few moments later, they went by again, but it was closed. No one was found in the attic apartment or on any other level in the building, and the doors were all locked securely from the inside. The salesman was as baffled by the strange door as Melissa was.

Melissa also told me that when they first bought the building, a couple times she had heard a baby crying up the stairs toward the bedrooms and attic apartment. Once she had been preoccupied with her paperwork when this happened and she had started to get up to see what was wrong before she realized that she was alone in the building. Being a mother herself, her natural inclination was to answer the distress cries of the infant, though no infant was in the building. In fact, Melissa was totally alone both times. Since then, she has not heard the infant's cries.

While talking to an employee who had worked for the former owners before Melissa and Shannon had taken over, the story of the baby's cry was once again mentioned. The employee was telling me that she had never had any ghostly experiences in the building, despite having worked there for more than ten years. She confessed too often feeling watched, but that was all. She paused for a second and thought. "You know the former owner's wife actually ran this place, like Melissa does. Now Mrs. ...... always said that this place was not haunted, but I know that she had several really odd experiences. She used to hear a baby crying upstairs when she was here early to catch up her paperwork, and several times she was working when the door to her office opened by itself and she heard someone walk in. She never saw anyone and she always kept her head down so that she wouldn't have to look up and see a ghost or something, but I know this really frightened her some."

The woman went on to relate how the one quilt on display in the dining room would pull itself out from the wall as if someone was looking at it, and at other times it shook and swayed despite there being no breeze.

She spoke of the dryer coming on by itself in the middle of the night, of footsteps in the dining room when there was no one there, of the table where the silverware would be found pushed into the center of the table when there were no customers. She told of many of the happenings that have often been reported.

Usually, I am the one reporting on other people's haunting experiences, but I believe that at the Jean Bonnet I also had an unearthly encounter. In September of 2000, I was going to give a Ghost Tour of Bedford County. I had been to the Jean Bonnet to arrange the details a couple weeks prior to the bus tour. Since I was already at the restaurant and it was past lunchtime, I decided to have lunch there. I was seated in the inner dining room and was happily munching my sandwich when I suddenly became aware that my left ear was freezing cold. It felt like someone had engulfed it in ice. My first thought was, "Man, they had better turn down the air conditioning!" But when I looked around, I realized that even if the air conditioning were on, it would not have been able to freeze that ear like that. I was facing away from the air and my left ear was near the wall, not the air conditioning.

I reached up to warm my ear and the earring, which felt icy, too. Suddenly, my hand was engulfed in a small, circular patch of cold air. I felt around it and it seemed to only radiate about 8 inches around my ear. Whatever it was, this cold spot was quite localized.

For several seconds, I continued to feel the area around the ear and still that cold spot just hung there. Perhaps the ghost was checking out my new earrings. For the rest of the day, my arm and hand would ache badly. I could not explain it, but where the cold spot had encountered my hand and arm I felt a dull, ache for about twelve hours. I could not explain it to myself at the time, and I can not explain it to you now. I do know that the air conditioning was not on because I asked my waitress to turn it off and she told me that it was not even on.

In late February of 2001 Scott, Crownover e-mailed me to let me know that he had stopped at the Jean Bonnet that night for supper and had been told of an incident that had occurred that very night. Everyone at the Jean Bonnet knows Scott, myself and a few others as the "ghost hunters," so when he came in, the manager, Barbara, came over and told him the story of an odd incident earlier that same night.

It seemed that a family that frequently came to the Jean Bonnet had been there that evening for supper. While they waited for their meal to be served in the tavern, the family's two-year old son was playing with his grandfather. The little boy would run into the hallway and come back. However, he went into the hallway one time and suddenly something at the top of the stairs caught his attention. Despite the fact that the child had never evidenced any fear in the building before, he now was very frightened. He claimed to have seen a "monster." The child was so upset that when they left he balked at passing the stairs again and his parents had to take him downstairs and out through the restaurant entrance.

The staff was concerned about the child's strange actions and insistence that he had seen a monster at the top of the stairs. When Barb spoke to the little boy's mother later in the evening, she inquired about the two-year old. His mother told Barb that the child was now fine. When they had questioned him at home about the incident, he said that he was not scared anymore, "because there are no monsters at home."

There are many stories of the ghosts at the Jean Bonnet, and I imagine that in some future book I'll, once again, return to the Jean Bonnet to tell you still more current stories. I can tell you that whoever is haunting the Jean Bonnet, and there seems to be many ghosts there, they are usually friendly. Most people who experience a haunting come away fascinated and not frightened. The owners, Melissa and Shannon Jacobs, are gra-

Jean Bonnet Photo from the Bedford Gazette Archive Provided by Melissa Jacobs

cious hosts and Shannon is the chef. The food is wonderful and the atmosphere relaxing and charming. No matter whether you are interested in ghosts or not, the Jean Bonnet is one restaurant and tavern that you really should visit. And if you do happen to have a ghostly experience, well don't forget to tell Melissa and me.

I would like to thank Melissa and Shannon for opening their business and their lives to my friends and me. We gratefully appreciate the hospitality and patience you have shown us. Because of your kindness, some of us, myself included, see the Jean Bonnet as a regular "haunt."

A HAUNTED COUNTRY CLUB

(Blair County)

The ------ Country Club has long been a fixture in Blair County. It existed before the turn of the Twentieth century. In the 1930's, it came to rest in its present building site. Scott Crownover invited me to come for a visit. Scott is a second-generation member, and grew up visiting this club. Through the years he learned many stories about the place, but the most interesting story came to him only recently, and that is that the club is haunted.

When Scott told me the story, he was only aware of one possible entity. However, after my visit and interviews with staff and patrons, I quickly came to realize that there are at least two spirits haunting the country club.

I first talked to an employee who told me that though she has never actually seen anything, she feels a presence in the building. She indicated the waitress station where the coffeepots and supplies are kept. She told me of a cook and other employees who had seen plates move and break for no reason. She repeated several of the stories that Scott had told me previously.

Everyone believes that the spirit they see and feel is that of *Paul, a former employee, who had committed suicide some time ago. Paul was the son of one of the long-time bartenders at the club and he had been head cook for years. To him the club was more than a job; it was a home away from home. He had helped remodel the building and painted parts of it. Paul had also ruled the kitchen with an iron oven mitt. He enjoyed his work, but he was a stickler for the rules. Once the grill was shut down and his kitchen cleaned, he would not reopen for tardy members. The rules were the rules for Paul.

What caused Paul to end his life, I do not know. Perhaps that is why he did not move on, but has returned to the kitchen where he loved to be in life.

One night, the present cook had just finished for the evening and shut down the kitchen. While he was in the bar, some of the members got hungry and he re-opened the kitchen to cook them some burgers and fixings. While he worked, two heavy skillet lids that lay on a shelf above the grill suddenly lifted themselves and were dropped on the floor. Now this was not merely heat forcing them to rise for several reasons. First of all, they were quite heavy and could not merely slide off. Secondly, these lids were picked up and flung far enough out that they missed the grill and the cook before dropping with a clatter. Those who knew Paul well immediately believed that he was upset that his rules about the kitchen being re-opened had been violated.

I spoke with a bartender who has worked at the club for twenty years. Michelle told me that she knew that the black shape of a man which she and many others have seen in the bar, walking through and disappearing into the hallway beyond could not be Paul because she has been seeing this man for years. She described what she sees as a tall, broad shadow of a man that moves through the old, original building. She knows her history of the club well. The club's present home was once a private residence belonging to a doctor. This home was purchased and turned into the bar. The lobby was once the front door area, and the hallway where the shadow disappears was part of the original building. Michelle told me that she believes that this shadow was the doctor who had lived there long ago. She told me that one night, she and two other women were in the bar talking when the shadow walked by them. One of the women piped up asking who had just passed. The bartender knew who it was, but declined to say anything. She felt validated, though, because all three women had seen the shadow.

Michelle told me that she and the other bartenders have all experienced this shadow figure. They have all, also, had other experiences that predate Paul's death. Quite often, late at night, they will hear loud banging coming from the kitchen. She described this sound as that of a metal pan falling or banging repeatedly onto the metal worktables. She said that when the bartenders investigate they never find anything out of place, nothing fallen, not even a metal pan sitting on the tables. Everything is neatly put away. One night, they even had the heavy metal coffee filter cup for a Bunn coffee maker shoot across the little waitress station and land near the wall. Now these things snap in, as I well know, and the idea of one falling, let alone shooting outward across a little room, is impossible. All of this reached the ears of the manager who doubted the entire story--until it happened to her. Now the manager does not scoff when a waitress or bartender talks about the pounding or other odd incidents because she has witnessed them for herself.

Michelle related another experience that happened when they were remodeling and painting some of the building. The paint cans, canvases, and ladders were stored on a little landing area on the stairs to the basement between the kitchen and waitress station. One evening she heard a can fall and roll down the stairs. She knew that the cans were not stacked up and the only way that one could fall over was if it was kicked or bumped. She finished getting the drink she was pouring while she thought, "Great, thanks Paul, now I'll have a mess to clean up." She thought Paul was responsible because the one area being repainted had been an area where he had remodeled before his death.

Not particularly pleased with the prospect of cleaning a mess of paint from the service stairs, Michelle hurried down them. Surprise was the only thing she found. Nothing was out of place. No can had rolled down the stairs; no paint was splattered about. The whole group at the bar had heard the loud noise, but there was nothing amiss.

Members have reported seeing the shadow figure, others have heard the thumps and many staff and some members have witnessed other phenomena as well. Through the glass windows between the bar and the main entrance, people have often seen someone come in. They wait for the person to get past the windows, but no one ever passes the other side.

Scott and I found low-level EMF readings localized in the kitchen area and a low-level reading in the basement where a fireplace still exists. However, whatever might be at this club seems most active after midnight. It is then that most people witness the shadow or hear the noises. Is this Paul returning to his old haunt from life, or is it the doctor coming and going in the wee hours as he must have in life? Perhaps a little of both as the bartenders believe. They noted that though there has been at least one death in the building during their tenure, the shadow predated that as well. They are not frightened by this entity, only mildly curious as to the identity.

Whatever walks through this country club is friendly and a bit quirky. These spirits seem to go about their business and only interact if rules are broken. Not one person I spoke to was afraid of them and I felt nothing frightening while I was there.

Though the ------- is a private club, they do have open nights from time to time and anyone who is interested in just sitting quietly and watching the bar late into the night might want to visit them then. Of course, there are no guarantees, and spirits are notoriously reticent about showing themselves to those who have come to see them.

A NIGHT AT TATESVILLE

(Tatesville, Bedford County)

I had always heard stories about a particular old railroad underpass near the small village of Tatesville, but stories passed on from generation to generation are notoriously unreliable. Still, often there seems to be some kernel of truth to them in the beginning. Therefore, I thought that a trip to Tatesville might be interesting if nothing else. I arranged for other members of the Central Pennsylvania Paranormal Association to come along. We were hopeful, but truthfully, I was not that optimistic.

I never tell the group members the stories of the sites we are to visit prior to their arrival, and often hold back critical details until later. I don't do that because I don't trust these people, because I do trust them and value the friendship of the other members. I withhold this information so that their observations won't be tainted by my stories. If there is a ghostly girl said to haunt a site, well, I don't want them to expect her or else the mind might put one there when there is not one. We human beings are all susceptible to this type of psychological persuasion. I know the history of most of the sites we visit and always feel that my observations are somewhat invalid unless others see them, too. I fear that I might be subtlety imagining things I have known should be there. If you don't think this is a valid concern, ask any police officer in the world about eyewitness accounts and they will tell you how unreliable they can be. Despite the fact that the American judicial system was founded upon the principal of eyewitness testimony, it still remains a fact that the human mind often perceives things in ways that are vastly different than reality.

I had been told the first story about this old railroad bridge underpass many years ago after moving to the area. The story began at the old Cypher Beach skating rink around 1969. Supposedly, a young girl about seventeen years old was there late one summer evening with her boyfriend. During the evening, something happened that upset the young girl and she and her boyfriend fought. When it was time to take her home, the argument continued. On the ride back, the girl suddenly got very angry and demanded to be let out of the car. The young man pulled over below the Union Cemetery and let her out. Though the young fellow did not like letting her out on this lonely stretch of road, what was he to do? He couldn't hold her hostage, could he? He comforted himself with the fact that she had only a short walk down the road through the underpass, to the stop sign and a little way beyond. Surely no more than a mile or a bit more; what could happen to her in a mile?

The young fellow returned home and went to bed. Late in the night, his mom awoke him to say that the girl's parents were on the phone. They wanted to know where their daughter was. The boy took the phone and explained about the fight and how she had demanded to be let out of his car. He told them where she had been dropped off, but he knew no more. By now, everyone was growing alarmed. Had the young girl simply gone off to sulk away her anger or had something happened to her?

The girl's parents and her boyfriend met and began driving the road from the spot where he had last seen her. No one saw a thing the first two times they went by. At last, they decided that they should walk the route just as she had. Who walked the road no one ever said, but that person saw a foot sticking out of a deep culvert on the right side of the underpass coming from the church. In the culvert, they discovered the crumpled body of the young girl hidden by thick summer vegetation. She had been raped and murdered. No one was ever prosecuted for this crime, but rumors have always swirled that the young girl is seen walking the road on the church side of the underpass. She supposedly hesitates as she nears the old stone railroad underpass and suddenly disappears.

After trying for many years to locate the actual people in this tale, I have to admit defeat. Does that mean that no one ever died there? No, I don't think so. Like so many of these stories, the facts are too vague for anyone to ever pin them down. I have been told often that it was in 1969, but others insist it was 1967, and still others that it was as late as 1972. It seems that something must have happened there, but it would take years of reading to pin down what happened and to whom.

At a tour I was giving, some local residents of the Tatesville area spoke up and said that they had always heard that a woman had hung herself from the bridge in despair. They insisted that locally it is claimed that in the late fall if you drive through the underpass late at night and look back in your rearview mirror you'll see the white, ghostly body of this woman swinging from the stone arch.

Now this story is sometimes tied to yet another tale that I was told by some folks in nearby Everett. According to this young man and his family, in the late 1950's a young woman got pregnant but she was not married. She managed to conceal the pregnancy and sneaked off into the woods to have the baby when the time came. Distraught because she did not want the child and fearful of what others would think, she stumbled to the top of the railroad underpass and tossed the innocent child from the high brink. The baby died instantly, but for years locals claimed to hear the thin, weak wails of a newborn at the underpass far into the morning hours. It was only an occasional event, but startling for those who had heard the child cry in this lonely spot where there are, even today, no houses close by.

With all of that in mind, I went to Tatesville. In the group were Scott Crownover, Mary, Becky, Carolyn and two curious local residents who tagged along. The day had been rainy and cloudy so I knew that few, if any of our results would be any good, yet I still wanted to go. By late afternoon, though, the rain had dried up and we were left with slightly misty conditions. Even this condition eased after we first got there.

Scott had his electromagnetic field (EMF) detector handy and began taking readings. On the right side of the underpass, coming from the church, there seemed to be electromagnetic field disturbance. Now there were no power lines, no homes, literally nothing we could see that would account for the spikes that moved along that side of the underpass. Scott climbed the slippery bank and found that near the top the readings were strongest. He snapped several photos when the EMF

Tatesville orb where the body was found

detector suddenly began to light up strongly. He tried to snap another photograph, but his camera suddenly was not working. He immediately called out, "Someone take a picture!" Everyone began snapping. Mary had a digital along with her 35 mm and she seemed to capture orbs in the photo Scott wanted.

As the evening progressed, Scott kept picking up readings on that side of the underpass where the girl was supposedly found. He also found strong readings at the very center of the underpass as high up as he could reach. Could that have anything to do with the stories of the young woman who had laced a rope around a tree, then placed the other end around her neck and jumped to her death there in the 1950's?

Throughout the evening Mary kept picking up orbs, and then she snapped a photo of what appears to be two almost human shapes on the side of the underpass where the EMF had been so strong. These white shapes did not appear on anyone else's film and were taken when there was no fog visible in the area, yet they are thick, distinct and nearly "human" in shape.

At one point Mary stepped back from the underpass and began rubbing her arms. "I'm just all creeped out," she said when I asked her what was wrong. Despite it being a warm summer night she was shivering. "Look," she said, holding out her arms; "I've got goose flesh." She seemed to be feeling the effect of something that was chilling her.

Just before we left, Scott got my attention and informed me that in the area immediately above where the culvert was, there seemed to be a glowing something moving about. The local residents who had joined us had pointed it out to him. Like myself, Scott had first thought of lightning bugs since we were there in the summer. However, we had not seen any that night. I watched the phenomena and sure enough a small light seemed to glow for an instant in one spot, wink out and begin glowing again in another spot only bare inches away. Several times I dove into the dirt and came up with a handful of dirt and leaves, but nothing else. On my fourth try, I bought up a handful of dirt, leaves, and phosphorescent larvae. I have never seen such bugs before, but this glowing light was coming from the little critters. Well, that goes to show that all that glows is not ghostly.

Still, when we left the underpass that night most of us felt that someone was there. In particular, Mary had captured many orb images and those two ghostly shapes. There was no mistaking the EMF readings, and the feeling that Mary had at one point that something was near her.

We would have one further little adventure that night. Just above the underpass is the Union church. I had an ulterior motive for stopping there. A woman had contacted me only weeks earlier to say that while researching her family genealogy she had inadvertently picked up a recording of her dead grandfather in that cemetery. Her family agreed that the voice on the tape was that of the dead man buried in that cemetery.

We stopped along the road and Scott played his thermal scanner and EMF over the large graveyard. Becky snapped a couple photos quickly, and then Scott called out that he had hit a 15-degree temperature drop and it was moving through the cemetery. As he followed it briefly with his thermal scanner, Becky and I snapped a couple more photos. Scott soon lost the temperature drop. We talked a few minutes before leaving. Only later would Becky realize that her first photograph of the church had captured supercharged energy. Apparently someone was watching us from the side of the church.

All in all, we had quite an adventure in Tatesville.

PHANTOM COAL MINERS

(Westmoreland County, Blair County and Cambria County)

Pennsylvania has long been associated with coal mining and the volatile and dangerous history that comes with it. Miners are not more superstitious than most folks are, but their constant proximity to death has had an impact. The many often needless and senseless deaths have given rise to many ghost stories. Here is a sampling of the tales I have collected.

It was a lovely morning, too lovely for walking to school, thought *Joleen as she and her older brother trudged along. Spring had finally come and she felt an urge to turn away from the school and go running through the forest that surrounded the trail. Still, her folks would not think kindly of her if she played hooky, so Joleen dutifully placed one foot after the other and kept to the path.

Joleen broke into a run to catch up to her big brother and, as she did so, she saw two figures walking along toward the school ahead of her. Though she couldn't see them well, she took them to be *Jack Maitland and his sister *Amanda.

"Come on," Joleen cried as she took off at a run; "Last one to reach Jack and Amanda is a rotten egg." With that she took off running, despite the fact that Joleen was 14 years old and her brother two years older, she felt childish today. She heard her brother pick up his pace behind her, but he did not start to run. "Stop that baby stuff," he scolded.

Still keeping her eye on Jack and Amanda who seemed unaware of the presence of the other children, Joleen dropped back and walked once more beside her brother.

Now the kids were in sight of the high school. To their surprise the figures that they had taken to be Jack and Amanda turned away from the school lane and turned in the opposite direction into the woods. Joleen and her brother stopped to watch this odd behavior. Suddenly, the two figures seemed to be sinking into the ground. They just faded downward until they were knee-deep in the ground, then their waists and their shoulders were swallowed up. Suddenly, they were gone. Whoever those two figures had been, they were not Jack and Amanda!

The siblings stood in silent shock for a few seconds. "Did you see that?" her brother breathed.

Joleen nodded. "They just disappeared. They sank down in the ground."

The brother and sister looked at each other in bewilderment. "I can't believe it," Joleen whispered.

Her brother looked at her, suddenly alert. "Yeah, well if you don't believe it and you just saw it, think about what other people will say. Don't tell anyone about this. They'll never believe us. You got that?"

Joleen nodded and she kept her promise not to tell.

For three years, neither sibling ever mentioned the strange event to anyone, but one day they were talking to an older neighbor about the area and the fellow told them that there had once been coal mines on the road between Latrobe and Derry. Both siblings perked up. This was the road they had been walking that day when they had seen the two mysterious figures.

The neighbor went on and said, "You know there's a patch of woods near the high school where there was once a mine collapse. About a 100 years ago, there was this big mine collapse out there and it was really bad. There were a lot of fellows down there, but they never got them out. The mine bosses said they were all dead, but there were lots of folks who didn't agree. They believed that some of those men at least, had to have been alive. Anyhow, the mine owners wouldn't allow the tunnel to be dug out and the bodies were never recovered. Don't know why they didn't at least put up a plaque or something, but to this day them bodies are down there just waiting for someone to dig them up."

With that Joleen looked at her brother. She did not say a word, but she knew that they were both thinking the same thing. She knew that they had seen two of the dead miners going to work that morning so long ago.

Since that time, the trees were cut down and a housing development was put up. However, no one ever spoke about the old miners buried there and Joleen felt it was best to keep her mouth shut. How could she tell anyone about the dead miners upon whom those new homes were built without telling the story of the two phantom miners whom she and her brother had seen in the mid-1970's?

The Night Miners

This story is more of a folktale than anything else. Most of the folks who could have verified this story for me have long since passed on, but I have had two separate folks tell me this story as it was told to them from an older relative, and amazingly, the stories meshed.

In Blair County there is an area roughly between Williamsburg and Martinsburg called Ormenia. This area was once a prosperous little community when it was a mining village. However, when the mines died out the people moved on and now only a few families are left in that area. There have long stood a row of wooden houses in the village and as these houses were owned by the mine and rented to employees, they became known as the row houses. Past the last row house was the mine opening. Today it can still be seen and there are still odd pieces of abandoned equipment from the mine strewn about, but time and nature are taking care of this. The mine is not safe and I do not recommend anyone poking around there. However, I have been told that through the years, several men died in the mines there. A few men died in cave-ins, but there were others who literally worked themselves to death and died of heart attacks within the mine. Perhaps these are the men I have been told about.

The family who lived in the last house nearest the mine long reported hearing odd noises from the closed mine late at night. They said that on occasion they'd see lights at the mine and figures moving about. Whenever anyone was called to check out the area, though, all would be quiet and the equipment was where it had been left when work had stopped at quitting time. Eventually, the family and their friends quit reporting the phantom men who seemed to be working the mine at night. No one believed them, anyhow. However, for those who had seen the lights and the men walking around, they did not care if they were believed, they knew that the mine was haunted by those who had sweated and died within the confines of that open pit.

The Haunted Mine on the Allegheny

This mine was located between Johnstown and Hollidaysburg on Allegheny Mountain and was known locally as the Patch Mine. It was a fairly large coal mine in its day and had a reputation for being haunted.

It was a normal night in the mines the night when the events that started the haunting occurred. The men were chipping away at the mountainside. Others picked up the lumps of coal and tossed them into the cars waiting nearby. The coal cars sat on a small track and were pulled by mules, ponies and strong horses. Each coal car weighted several tons when fully loaded. That night no one noticed that the line attaching one of the heavily loaded cars to its horse was weak. When the horse began it's journey back topside with the heavy load, it made it most of the way up the track before the line broke and the loaded coal car began to roll backward. As it went, it picked up speed until it was careening along. Downward the car screamed until it slammed into several miners and their mules that had not seen it coming in time to get off the tracks.

Suddenly it was not a normal night in that mine anymore. It was a very unusual and tragic one. Every one of the several miners and their mules lay dead. Some literally cut in two by the weight and speed of that coal car.

After that night the shaft where the tragedy had occurred was to be closed for a bit. It had been an old shaft and the owners knew that no one would venture into that shaft after the deaths, so they ordered two men to close it up.

Both of the men the mine boss chose for this task were new to the company and did not know the history of that shaft. The mine boss did not want any ghost stories starting up. Ghost stories were bad business inside of a mine.

For six nights, the two men worked at walling up the side shaft. They noticed that the other miners weren't very friendly. No one talked to them as they worked.

One of the two fellows was a bit of a slacker and he'd take whatever opportunity offered itself for a bit of a nap. The fellow liked his booze and the ladies better than work, so he opted to sleep at work.

On their first day, the lazy fellow told his buddy that he was going to take a nap while the other man worked on. Though it wasn't fair and the hard worker wasn't thrilled about it, he didn't want to cause any trouble. So, the lone man worked on in the twilight. He noticed that he kept hearing noises that were already familiar to him. It was the distinct sound of a horse wheezing it's last raspy breaths. Having grown up around animals it was a common enough noise, but where was it coming from?

The hard worker began to wonder just where that sound was coming from. He located an area where the sound was strongest, but there was nothing there! The man noticed that every time he heard this sound it was just before lunchtime. For the whole six days, the hard worker heard that odd wheezing sound just before lunch break. If that were the only sound he heard, he would have long forgotten the story. However, one day he heard someone walking down the shaft and into another shaft that he knew very well had long been blocked off. It was not easy to mistake sounds down there. The clink, clink of the picks, the clomp, clomp of the ponies and mules and the slushy sound of men in rubber boots were all quite distinctive and he knew he heard a man walking.

The hard worker kept his thoughts to himself about the mineshaft. He later found out exactly what had happened down there, but he never volunteered the story of the horse dying nor of the man who walked through sealed shafts.

One day his mine boss took him aside and asked him directly if he had heard any odd noises down in the mine. Being asked directly made the miner decide that he'd better tell the truth. He confessed to hearing the sounds of a horse dying and to the sloshing steps of a miner in the closed shaft.

The mine boss looked depressed and shook his head. He told the worker that it was just what he was afraid of. There was a fortune in coal down that shaft, but they would not be able to touch it because no one would work in that haunted shaft. For as long as that man worked the mines, no one ever ventured to enter the haunted shaft. As far as we know, that fortune in coal may still lie sealed within the mountainside, protected by a spectral miner and his dying horse

The Coal Miner of the Inclined Plane

Johnstown is known for the history surrounding the several tragic floods that took place there, but I have never come across one haunting in the area from those tragic events. I am told that there are ghosts at the memorial park, but I have no specific stories to pass on. However, there is another tale from Johnstown's often-tragic history that has spawned a ghost.

Perhaps one of the most underrated dangers faced by miners were the dangers of gases. Natural gases could poison them all or even cause an explosion if ignited.

Where today there is the Inclined Plane hillside, in 1902 there was a thriving mine. However, despite the best precautions taken by the miners, they must have hit a large pocket of natural gas and a spark set it off. The explosion was massive and 115 men died instantly in that roaring surge of flame.

However, if reports from the area are accurate, at least one of the dead miners has been returning to the surface. There are reports that a miner in early 1900's clothing has been seen going up the hiking trail at the base of the Inclined Plane. Is he returning to work or trying to return home? Since no one knows exactly who this phantom miner is, we can not know why he is still traveling a path to somewhere.

The story of mines and ghostly miners will continue as long as men are forced to crawl beneath the ground to rob the earth of her riches. What a terrible job it must be to stay buried beneath the earth for endless hours. No wonder miners believe so strongly in their ghosts!

OUIJA

One thing that I have been asked about repeatedly during my lectures is my belief about ouija boards. Through the years, I have studied this topic quite seriously and I agree with every expert on this topic from leading psychiatrists to leading psychics who all agree that ouija boards should not be considered toys. I have had several people confide their stories of experiences with ouija boards, and I thought that I'd share some of them with you here.

The Unwelcome Visitor

*Marlene sat beside the ouija board at her mother's kitchen table and coaxed her older sister, *Gerry to play. Neither of them were little girls anymore. Marlene was 23 and Gerry 25 years old, married and pregnant. Marlene continued to wheedle at her older sister. "Come on, Gerry, you know that things always happen when we play together."

Gerry shook her head hesitantly. On one hand, she did enjoy the excitement and energy that came from the board, but she did not enjoy other side effects that sometimes came with it. "I don't want to start those noises up again," she muttered more to herself than to Marlene. Gerry tried not to think of the scratching and stomping noises that had filled the house for hours after the last session.

Marlene sighed. "Chicken! They were just noises. They couldn't hurt you. Come on; let's see what it has to say."

Gerry allowed herself to be persuaded and she reluctantly sat down. "Okay, but only for a little while, and if you agree to stop if anything unusual happens?"

Marlene nodded her consent. "We'll stop if you get scared."

Gerry sat down and reluctantly placed her fingers on the planchette. "Okay, but..." her voice faded away as they began to work. When she touched a ouija board, it always seemed to just work for her.

Marlene asked who was there as the planchette moved about with their fingers barely touching it.

In response, the planchette moved to the "J." Then it moved to "A," and on it went until it had spelled "James."

Gerry kept her hand on the planchette and she gave a little unconscious sigh. "James" was a nice normal name.

"Do you have a message?" Marlene asked.

"We will come." The board spelled each letter.

Gerry did not like the sound of that. She thought about pulling her fingers away from the board but Marlene was so intensely into the conversation that she knew her sister would be angry.

"Who will come?" Marlene demanded.

The planchette slid to the word "No" and stopped.

Marlene slid forward, "Is there anyone else who wants to come through?"

The board was silent. No movement came from the planchette.

"Is there anyone else who wants to come through?" Marlene repeated her request.

Suddenly the door of the oven behind Marlene flew open. At the same time there were heavy footfalls on the stairs leading to the apartment. Gerry pulled her hand away and jumped up. "That's enough," she cried as she grabbed for the door. She had to be sure someone was really coming up the stairs.

No one was there! Gerry observed the empty hallway with trepidation. Her parents lived on the second floor of a large, old house in Altoona. The only place anyone could go when they mounted the stairs was into the apartment or down the hall to the attic where both families had storage space. She looked at the attic door and knew it would do no good to try it. The door was always locked and the old lady who lived in the first floor apartment never went up there. She could no longer negotiate steps.

Gerry stepped back into the apartment. "I'm not going to do that anymore," she told Marlene sternly. "No matter what you say I'm not touching that thing again, so don't ask." She pointed at the ouija board lying on the table.

Marlene wrinkled her nose as she began to put away the board. "You're a fraidy cat! It's just a game you know, and besides don't you really wonder if there is anything out there?"

Gerry shook her head. "No, I don't. I know there's something out there and I don't want to meet it, at least not right now."

The rest of the afternoon went well and when her husband, *Jon came to pick her up, Gerry did not mention playing the board to him. She had told him about the last time and they had agreed that she'd let the thing alone. She would have kept her promise, too, if it hadn't been that Marlene had nagged her so badly.

****

Gerry struggled awake as the phone rang. It was barely 7 a.m. and she was tired. She was always tired now that her due date was so near. Everyone knew she needed rest so who could have been calling her?

"Hey, you're not going to believe what happened last night!" Marlene's voice was excited, but there was also an unfamiliar edge to it. Was she frightened?

Gerry sat up in bed and pushed her hair back. "What happened? What's wrong?" She was barely awake.

"Do you remember those heavy footsteps that we heard when we were just about done playing the ouija board yesterday?"

Gerry mumbled that she did. Suddenly she was wide-awake.

"About 10 o'clock last night we all went to bed. We couldn't have been in bed more than a few minutes before we heard them pounding up and down. Dad and Mom got up several times to see who was there, but when they'd open the apartment door no one was there. Then we began hearing a baby cry. It was a real loud crying like the baby was right next door or something. I looked out the window, but no one was outside with a baby. And you know that there are no babies in this neighborhood right now."

With those words Marlene described what would be several weeks of bad haunting for the family. The heavy footsteps tread the boards nightly, and the incessant crying of an infant kept sounding both day and night. The cries seemed to come from a room in the apartment, but whenever they tried to locate the source it would move. One day they managed to trace the cries into the kitchen when suddenly there was a terrible knocking on the oven door. Marlene and Gerry's mother had grabbed open the oven only to hear loud cries from a child inside. Somehow this seemed so sinister and unnerving to the whole family that they stopped looking for the child after that.

But perhaps the worst part of the haunting came when the family began to see a woman in a white or pale blue nightgown walking the halls and in the bedrooms. One night their teenaged brother even awoke to see the woman watching him sleep. He refused to sleep in that room for days.

Each day Gerry's husband would bring her to her family home before work and she'd wait out the day regretting the fact that she had allowed Marlene to bait her into using the ouija board. The family kept the haunting activity to themselves and finally, they decided to ignore it in hopes that it would just go away. Eventually it finally did taper off, but occasionally there are still footsteps or the troubled cries of an infant, and a few relatives have reported seeing a woman in white at the head of the stairs when they have entered the building.

There had been no haunting in this house prior to the use of the ouija board. Indeed, it did seem that when "James" had said "We are here." he meant it.

The Unburnable Board

In many forms and ways I have heard this story time and again. I have to say that I've never owned a ouija board, and so I've never had occasion to burn one. However, at least three different people have told me of their troubled experiences with a board they tried to destroy after having an unnerving event happen to them.

*Kelly James looked at the ouija board her best friend *Sally had just taken out of the closet. She felt fear clutch her heart. "I don't think we should mess with that," Kelly ventured.

Sally just laughed and laid the board on the bed. "I know your mom's really religious, Kelly, but honestly, it's just a toy! Look," she flipped the board over and Kelly saw the Parker Brothers Logo on it. "Do you think they could really sell this thing if it was for real?"

Kelly shrugged and picked up the directions. At age seventeen she had never been near a ouija board before. Her mother was not just religious, she was very religious, and if she knew that Kelly was anywhere near this thing she'd have gone ballistic. Still, Kelly did not want to seem different to her friends, so she went along with things.

Sally sat up the board and explained it to Kelly. "It's really very simple. Since there are only two of us, we each put our fingertips on this thingy," she indicated the planchette. "We don't push or anything, just let them rest there, then we ask questions. The thingy will move and we just have to keep our fingertips on it while it does so that the connection is not broken."

Sally smiled at the uncertain look on Kelly's face. "You're not gonna get possessed or anything you know, but" she added slyly, "you might find out if Brad is going to ask you out."

Stupid as it would later seem, Kelly thought that was a good enough reason why she should go along--that and peer pressure.

The girls asked the board several questions and to Kelly's amazement the planchette really did seem to move on it's own--or was it Sally who was pushing it along? Kelly couldn't tell, but she knew that she wasn't pushing it; she was barely touching it at all.

Brad was going to ask her out, or so the board said. The two girls giggled over that and the answers to several more questions. Kelly had lost most of her fear of the thing by now. It really was just a fun game--at least if Sally was the one controlling it.

"Where am I going to be when I'm twenty?" Sally asked.

"DEAD." The board replied.

Sally looked at Kelly. "That's not funny!" she cried.

"I'm not doing it, I thought you were." Kelly jerked her hand away.

Sally grabbed Kelly's wrist and forced it back toward the planchette. "No, I'm asking that question again."

Reluctantly Kelly put her hand back on the planchette.

"Where will I be when I'm twenty years old?" Sally's voice held an edge.

"DEAD." Again the board spelled.

Kelly wanted to stop but Sally refused.

"How will I die?" she whispered.

Once more the planchette took off beneath their fingers.

"BURN." The letters spelled out.

Now Sally pulled her fingers away from the offending board as if she had already been burned. "Let's quit, it's not fun anymore."

The girls packed up the board and laid it back on the shelf in the closet. The two girls tried to recapture the light feeling of earlier in the evening, but it now eluded them. Finally, the two girls decided to go to sleep.

In the darkness, just before they drifted off to sleep, a thud sounded. It came from the closet.

"Did you hear that?" Kelly whispered into the darkness.

"Yes." Sally sat up and turned on the bedside lamp. She opened the closet door and the ouija board fell out at her feet. Both girls gave a little cry, but they ended it with a giggle.

"We must not have put it on the shelf right." Kelly picked up the pieces and reboxed it. Carefully they laid the board flat upon the shelf and softly closed the door.

They both lay back down and talked for a few minutes. Suddenly their conversation was interrupted by a soft thud from the closet. Once more the girls got up and turned on the lights. With real trepidation now, Kelly opened the closet door. The board fell out and landed at her feet. She gave a little squeal and jumped backward as if the board was a living thing.

Sally sat up in bed with large, round eyes. "Put it on the floor, Kelly. It wants us to use it again, but I don't want to know more."

Kelly picked up the board and boxed it up again. Now she was feeling sick in her stomach. It had never occurred to her to question Sally's assertion for it was her own belief as well.

Carefully, she slid the box back into the closet on the floor by a pair of sneakers. "It'll be okay there," she told Sally with more authority than she felt.

The girls once more lay down, but now they didn't talk at all. The darkness seemed oppressive. Kelly couldn't sleep, but Sally was so quiet that she wondered if her friend had dozed off.

Kelly froze. There was a thumping sound coming from the closet. Both girls sat up and looked at each other, then the closet.

"Do you hear that," Sally whispered. The two girls stepped toward the closet together. As Kelly reached for the doorknob, they held each other's hand.

The box was where Kelly had left it next to the sneakers, but now it was softly bouncing up and down. The rattle of the planchette inside was what had made the soft thump.

For a second, the girls just looked at the box doing the impossible little dance in the closet. Suddenly, Sally reached down and grabbed it up. "Come on," she whispered grabbing Kelly's hand.

The girls pulled on their shoes and Sally stopped in the kitchen just long enough to snatch up a box of matches and the starter fluid for the grill that was kept on a high shelf in the pantry.

Together, they went outside and across the yard to where the burn barrel stood. Sally tossed the box inside and Kelly squirted some lighter fluid on it. Sally struck a match and dropped it on the box. For a few brief seconds the box caught fire and flared up quickly. The fluid gave the fire a burst and the box burned.

The girls watched as the thing burned up. "Now, that's done," Sally said with satisfaction. The girls returned to their room.

The next morning both girls went back to the burn barrel to see if anything was left of the board. As they poked into the ashes with a stick, they immediately realized that the instructions and box had burned, but the board, though singed, was still intact.

Fear gripped their hearts. The board was made of particleboard and should have burned well. The planchette was plastic, but it had not melted. Perhaps the fire was not hot enough or had not lasted long enough. The girls tried again. This time they burned bags of garbage around the board, but still it resisted destruction.

When the ashes had cooled enough to poke through, the girls again found the board burned, but in tact. They fished it out of the fire and decided to break it up. They hit it with hammers and dropped rocks on it. Now they were truly frightened. It should have been destroyed long ago.

Finally, Sally looked at Kelly. "Your mom," she said, "What would she do with something like this?"

Through bloodless lips Kelly answered. "She'd pray."

"Then do that," Sally whispered back.

Kelly did not exactly pray, she began reciting Bible verses and at last, Sally was able to break the board in two with a hammer. As Sally splintered the board, Kelly kept repeating the few verses she knew over and over. After that, they burned the board easily.

From that day on Kelly has never touched a ouija board. In fact, she now has a very dim view of them.

Years have gone by and Sally did not die in a fire or any other way. She's now 23 years old and married. However, both girls believe that the intent of this board was to frighten and intimidate them.

"GO TO HELL!"

This story came to me from a woman who used the board as a teenager. She was of the opinion that the boards were just for fun and had scoffed at her mother who had insisted that the boards were occultic. However, after a slumber party she had changed her mind. (In this story some information has been changed, but not the actual event.)

*Susan was the type of girl who always did what she was not supposed to. When her mother forbid her to date boys at age sixteen, she did it secretly. When her mother counseled her not to go out with *Frank Thayer because he was "a wild one," she felt even more drawn to him. They dated and, after Susan announced that she was pregnant, Frank tried to leave her. Still Susan did not learn her lesson, so when one evening a girlfriend named Lynn brought over a ouija board to kill the hours she thought it sounded like fun.

She knew very well that her mother had always told them that those boards were of the devil, but Susan did not buy that story. It was a bunch of religious claptrap.

The young women set up the board and began to play. It was working well. Each young woman suspected the other of pushing the planchette across the board, and they giggled at the answers to their silly questions.

"Your turn," Lynn told Susan.

"Okay..." Susan paused to think up a good question. She was tired of silly things like who will I marry. "I know," she looked directly at the board and said, "Are you good or bad?"

The planchette moved to "No."

"That doesn't make sense," Susan muttered. "It didn't answer me."

Once more she addressed the board. "Are you from Heaven or Hell," she asked the entity whom they had been conversing with.

Again the planchette moved to "No."

"Are you from Heaven or Hell," Susan demanded yet again.

"GO TO HELL." The planchette spelled out.

Susan felt a terrible thread of fear, but she also felt a determination that she had never felt before. She needed an answer. It really defied logic, but she just felt at that moment that she had to have a straight answer. "Are you from God or Satan," she demanded.

"BURN IN HELL" the planchette spelled out and slid to the edge of the board. After that, it would not work.

Susan felt, though, that her question was more than adequately answered and she told me that she never again touched a ouija board.

Again, I am asked about ouija boards at nearly every lecture and book signing I do. Every reputable psychic I've ever spoken with has told me that they feel these devices can be dangerous in the hands of certain people. Those who have low-level psychic ability and who don't recognize it as such can call in spirits, both good and bad with the use of such a device. I have heard stories of everything from possession to sudden hauntings, to a family in Canada who was actually badly beaten, bit and scratched and ended up in the hospital. This family all told the same story of using a ouija board and making contact before there were suddenly lights shooting around the room and they were being physically attacked by something they could not see.

If even half of the stories are true and if the ministers and psychics I have spoken with are accurate, you must remember that for certain people these boards could be dangerous or at least very frightening. By using this board it is as if you are standing at a door and shouting "Come in," before you even look to see who may be on the other side.

PERHAPS A GHOST STORY?

(Blair County)

Though I am about to relate this story for you, I can not promise you that it is a ghost story. I can only promise you that it truly happened and that it is to this day an enigma. Because there are several folks in the same town with names similar to that of the man that this happened to, I've opted to change the man's name.

*George Berk picked up the clipboard on the battered old desk in the borough building and flipped through it. His eyes rested for a few seconds upon one particular work order. It was one he often had. George worked as a water works operator for a small town in Blair County and part of his job was turning on, turning off and maintaining the water meters in town. Through the years he had held his job he had noticed that one house seemed to be moved into and out of repeatedly. It was a puzzle to him why this house had such a turnover. It was a lovely red brick house with three bedrooms, right on the edge of town and near the largest employer in town. It was beautiful inside, and though he had heard that it was difficult to heat, he couldn't imagine that someone had not had the foresight to purchase insulation and redo the house rather than moving on.

George tucked the battered clipboard into the toolbox he was carrying and deposited it all on the bench seat of the old, red Ford pick-up that the borough used. He'd seen no special instructions for that red brick house, so he decided to put that job off until the afternoon. He'd start on the other side of town with a water main that needed flushed and move on, making a circuit and catch the red brick house on his way back.

By the time George got to the house it was nearly 3 p.m. He quit at 3:30 p.m., but he felt that he had plenty of time to go down to the basement and turn on the water before going back to the borough building.

He picked up the clipboard off the seat and his toolbox and got out. For a second, he studied the house and sighed. There were no cars in the driveway. Now that was a bad sign. Still, he was already here, so maybe there was someone home and it was a one-car family. He might as well give it a shot.

George stepped up onto the cement porch and rang the bell. He was wondering once again why this particular house had such a high tenant turnover. Of course, he had often wondered about it in recent years. He must have turned the water on and off a dozen times in the past two years alone. He gave the doorbell another push and waited, but now he wasn't very hopeful.

Just as George was about to turn and leave, he heard shuffling from inside the house and he made out the figure of an old woman coming toward the door slowly. This was new, he thought. Usually the couples that rented the house were young and he had figured that this one was no exception judging from the toys on the porch. Still, maybe it was a mother or grandmother who lived with them. In fact, it didn't matter as long as the lady could let him in and sign the paper when he was done.

The woman opened the door and stared at him, but she didn't say anything.

"Afternoon, ma'm, I'm from the borough; you called to have your water turned on today?"

The old woman nodded but still did not say anything. Not very talkative George thought, but then again that might be just fine as it was nearly quitting time and usually old ladies held him up chatting because they were lonely.

The woman nodded at him and turned making a motion for him to come along. He followed her to the kitchen where the basement door was. He didn't say anything, but he already knew the way.

At the door, the old woman stepped aside and with a "thank you" George went downstairs.

He had finished adjusting the meter and turning it back on when he heard the sound of a woman and children upstairs. The basement door opened and a woman called down, "Who's down there?" There was suspicion and fear in her voice.

George hastened to step into the wedge of light made by the door and introduced himself. "I'm George Berk from the borough, ma'am. I just come to turn your water back on. You called. I got the work order right here." He reached down and scooped up the clipboard.

The woman stepped back as George came up the stairs toward her. As soon as he had safely passed her and was at the front door, she followed him.

"I need you to sign here; ma'am to say I turned it on." George held out a pen and the board for her.

The woman looked at him in distain. "I ought not to sign that. In fact, I should probably call the police on you. I don't care if you are from the borough; you had no right breaking into my house when I wasn't home. You could have waited a couple minutes. I only went to pick the kids up at school!"

Now George was getting a bit angry. Break in, indeed! Hell, he had been let in and probably by this smart-mouthed young woman's mother or something. He was mad and he told her so.

When he mentioned the old woman, however, the lady only grew angrier. "I don't know whom you're talking about, but there's no one of that description living here. It's just my husband, the kids and me. If you're planning to lie to get out of trouble, you'll have to do better than that!"

George looked the woman square in the eye, still holding the clipboard out to her. "Lady, I don't know who the old woman was, but I saw an old woman! She let me in and led me to the basement door. I went down there and she went somewhere else. Now, sign this or let me get out of here."

The woman signed the form and shut the door, but she seemed to be still very upset.

George wasn't feeling any better. If that young woman was telling the truth and there were no old women living in the house, then who had let him in? George thought that now he had a pretty good idea just why so many folks moved out of that house.

About ten years after this incident happened to George, the house was torn down and the lot was landscaped as part of a larger property. The owner insisted that he couldn't keep tenants, but he never mentioned why. Is it a ghost story? You decide!

THE IRON KETTLE

(Camp Hill, Cumberland County)

Those who have read the first volume of the Ghost Guide will be familiar with Kelly Weaver. Kelly is a professional psychic from Camp Hill, PA. I met Kelly while working on the first volume of the Ghost Guide. I went to interview Kelly as a skeptic, but came away convinced that she is one of those rare people who really do have the abilities she claims to possess. Since that time, what I have observed has only strengthened my belief that she is for real. The following story is one of the very first ones she ever shared with me. I subsequently spoke to the owners and they confirmed Kelly's story.

The Iron Kettle is a restaurant in the industrial section of Camp Hill. It looks much like the buildings around it and certainly blends into the area, but the similarity ends there. The Iron Kettle is another world on the inside. The atmosphere is one of country charm and casual elegance. You would find yourself at home in nice jeans or a dress suit. The owners, Mr. and Mrs. Beshove work hard to keep the service and food up to the high standards that they have set through the years.

The building has been in Mrs. Beshove's family for forty years. She and her husband have run the business for 24 yrs. now. They know that the building has long had a reputation within the family and among the staff for haunting phenomena. Among the most common reports are stories of someone whistling or making train sounds in the warehouse area, and of pots and pans clanging or moving when no one is near them.

Kelly first learned of the haunting in the building while she worked at her previous job as a sales representative for a local newspaper. While she was there to sell space in the local paper to the restaurant, she happened to mention that she could tell that the building was haunted. The Beshoves invited Kelly back to their establishment to tell them more. They were interested to hear what she might tell them about the resident ghosts.

Kelly and a friend from her group, who is also psychic, toured the restaurant and noted their impressions. It was amazing how similar their accounts were--unless you do believe in psychics.

They picked up on two older men. One fellow did not give them a name and was grumpy with them. He seemed upset that the other spirit was there, too. However, the second spirit, "Clarence" was different. He was an alcoholic in life who had also had a passion for the trains he had worked with to earn his living. Kelly believes that Clarence is responsible for much of the phenomena in the first floor. Perhaps Clarence enjoyed visiting the Iron Kettle in his life, so he returned to a favorite watering hole after death.

In the kitchen the two psychics felt children. The kitchen is a happy place with the bustle of activity. There is a group of children there from some time in the past, Kelly told me. The children are active and they are the ones who move things and bang the pans around when no one is in the room. Kelly saw three little girls and a little boy ghost in the kitchen. They move as shadows, but are rarely seen. It is more often just a feeling that they are around. Sometimes Mr. Beshove will catch a glimpse of something when he's alone in the building in the morning.

There have been reports of other childish phenomena happening to Mr. Beshove. His wife told me that he has had the television set turned on and has been tickled while alone in the building. Two kitchen workers reported to the Beshoves that one day they saw an item on a shelf move itself around. That was enough for them, they left the area for a bit.

In the warehouse, people have reported hearing a train whistle sound being mimicked, and one bartender said she heard a scream when she went in for some bottles of liquor. Mrs. Beshove once heard the scream as well, and she admitted that it was disconcerting.

Doors have been known to open by themselves. There have been strange lights flash in the dining room. Kelly's husband John has taken photographs of ectoplasmic mist near the jukebox. The jukebox is in an area where a few people have reported suddenly feeling very sad. This is the only truly sad spot in the building, but it only occasionally affects anyone.

There are two apartments above the restaurant and Kelly discovered another entity up there. This fellow was an old man who used to live in the building. Mrs. Beshove found Kelly's words disconcerting. Kelly asked who the man was and suddenly numbers began tumbling through her head. The number 7 seemed forceful. When Mrs. Beshove heard this, she immediately remembered that both of her parents had died on the 7th of the month and her father had lived in that apartment at the end of his life. She was worried that for some reason his spirit was trapped in the building. However, it could well be that Mrs. Beshove's father has remained behind to watch over the family business.

Mrs. Beshove went to the county courthouse to look up the history of the ground where the Iron Kettle now sets. She traced it back to the mid-1800's. It was then a farm and a farmhouse, outbuildings and perhaps a couple tenant houses were on the property. In the 1920's, the ground was the site of Hunt Car Motors. The present building was built around 1954 to house two businesses on the first floor and with an apartment on the second floor for rent.

For the Beshoves and Mrs. Beshove's family, the ghosts are only part of the charm of the building. They are not anxious to remove the ghosts, but they do hope to understand them better. If you're ever in the Camp Hill area and have the time, go visit the Iron Kettle and see if you experience any of the haunted phenomena for yourself.

Kelly Weaver can be contacted at
43 Essex Road
Camp Hill, PA 17011
www.kellysmagicalgarden.com

THE POWWOW MAN AND THE GHOST OF REUBEN ROCK

(Claysburg, Blair County)

I owe a debt of thanks to a local family from Bedford County who shared the unusual history of their grandfather with me. In the process, they gave me a great local ghost story. You'll think so too, after reading this!

Could Witchcraft ever really have been afoot in Blair and Bedford Counties? Was Witchcraft practiced in Pennsylvania in the 1940's? Who would have believed it was possible in those two rural counties where life is usually filled with family and church life? Yes, occasionally the world does impose itself in the guise of violence or cruelty, but the idea of witchcraft, of curses, and the dead coming back to hound the living just does not seem logical. Yet, that is exactly what happened in the little town of Claysburg at the close of World War II. And if the story is true, and it seems that it is, then witchcraft and curses did affect one family.

Rosella Dively and Reuben Rock were young lovers. He and the young Rosella fell in love and were married just prior to his being shipped out during World War II. Reuben Rock served through several north Africa campaigns, but he contracted tuberculosis and was sent back to Bull's Creek in the spring of 1946. Reuben and Rosella began their life together. They set about building a little home in Claysburg, but this construction was halted repeatedly by Reuben's illness.

Reuben Rock   *Rosella Rock*

*Home of Reuben Rock
Altoona Mirror archive*

When the tuberculosis would lay him up, Rosella would lovingly take care of him in the two rooms on the first floor of the little house that were the most complete. This was not the future that the young couple had planned. It was not the future that had sustained Rosella through the long wait for Reuben to return. Still, he had returned and there was hope.

However, after several bad bouts with the lung disease, Rosella had to know that Reuben was not going to make it. The stress was terrible for Rosella, and anyone with a heart can imagine what it must have been like for the young bride.

Reuben died on January 13th at the age of 29. Rosella found herself a 22-year-old widow. She had many decisions to make now and she threw herself into the funeral preparations as a last act of love for her dear husband.

Reuben had given her his Army uniform upon his return, but upon his deathbed he had told her he never wanted to wear it again. Rosella, however, believed that Reuben's sacrifice should be honored. He had died for his country as assuredly as any man who had been shot down in the heat of battle. Reuben's sacrifice had been long and painful and this needed to be remembered. Rosella decided to bury him in the uniform and American Legion post 522 gave him a full military funeral.

After Reuben's death Rosella's family grew very concerned for her. She seemed inconsolable. She did not eat or sleep and her mother grew greatly concerned for her own daughter's safety. When her mother came to Rosella's little unfinished house, she found books and papers that led her to believe that Reuben had been interested in witchcraft and voodoo while in Africa. She knew that in the end Reuben had spoken to a minister, but now those papers upset her greatly. In an interview with Rosella's mother that ran in the Altoona Mirror, she is quoted as saying, "Rosella began worrying about a picture of her that Reuben had carried... He was saved at the end, but he had books and things in his house. Rosella was just crazy to be with him. She would probably go to him at any time. That's probably how he did it, by charming her picture that he always carried with him. After he died, Rosie just started wasting away."

Rosella's mother decided that this picture that Reuben had always carried needed to be located. She dispatched family members to look through Reuben's possessions and it was found by one of Rosella's brothers. Attached to the picture frame was a rabbit's foot. There was also a little pamphlet and other papers that upset the family. Rosella's brother brought the photograph back to the house where he laid it on the table before his mother.

When Rosella's mother took the photo from the frame, according to the family, the photo frame literally crawled in her hands. Rosella's family began praying and Rosella's brother burned the frame so that no curse would befall them.

With that they all thought that Rosella would be okay, but once she returned to her little house things got worse. She heard someone knocking on the ceiling, saw Reuben's face in the windows, and heard walking when she was alone. Worse yet, others also experienced the haunting. Reuben was literally driving Rosella to a nervous breakdown.

Among the items in the box with the charmed picture and frame was a religious tract that the family now looked at. It was from a man named Edward Culp Ferguson of rural Bedford County. He billed himself as a gospel worker and healer, but many locals knew him as a powwow man.

In desperation, the family contacted Ferguson. After coming to speak to the family a few times, Ferguson determined that Reuben was upset with Rosella for burying him in his military uniform. The solution for this was simple to Ferguson; he'd exhume the body, perform a cleansing ritual and rebury the corpse.

On February 22, the Divelys, the gravedigger and Ferguson went to the cemetery and began the exhumation. At 7 a.m., they disinterred the body and Ferguson had Reuben removed from the casket. The uniform was taken off. The body was sprinkled with salt and wrapped in white sheets. Then it was returned to the grave. With that, the haunting of Rosella Rock ended.

Edward (Culp) Ferguson provided by the family

Reuben Rock grave site

Are there curses? Can powwow men really lay the dead and ease a restless spirit? Today we laugh at such things, but apparently it worked in the case of Reuben Rock!

THE GHOSTS OF THE
FULTON OPERA HOUSE

(Lancaster, Lancaster County)

During the summer of 2000 I was invited by my friend Becky Gummo to join her and another friend, Al Brindza, their spouses and Al's son and a guest for a late-night visit to the Fulton Opera House. I fell in love with that place. The beauty of the theater is breathtaking and the Victorian charm dazzled me, but, of course, I also was impressed with their ghosts. How ironic it turned out to be that such beauty lay atop an evil deed done long ago in Lancaster's past, yet not forgotten.

To understand the Fulton Opera House you must understand that it is an amalgam of the history of both Lancaster County and Victorian Theater. Perhaps one of the most tragic and senseless events in the history of Pennsylvania took place in the basement of the old Lancaster jail long before the Opera house was ever built. Yet this event was so heinous and so tragic that it has left a lasting impression on both the state and the Fulton Opera House that would be built on the site of the old jail.

In 1763, Chief Pontiac was waging war across Ohio and Pennsylvania. He was fighting to drive back the tide of whites who had not only invaded native lands, but who had also embarked upon a policy of death or destruction for natives throughout the entire northeast. The whites did not understand nor did they care why the natives were rising up. This was in a time when the trumped up concept of Eminent Domain held sway. At this time, the only good Indian was a dead Indian and that was a sentiment generally felt even in William Penn's Pennsylvania.

White soldiers had raided many Indian villages throughout the state by this point. The white soldiers had pursued a scorched earth policy that meant that they burned crops, storehouses, and homes. They killed or drove out the Indians from their homes and took scalps and other body parts as souvenirs. This was a large part of why Chief Pontiac rebelled against white rule.

The British government in Philadelphia under the leadership of Governor James Hamilton refused repeated requests for troops to protect the frontiers, for weapons and ammunition, and for any other help. By help, the frontiersmen meant troops to burn and kill.

Because Governor Hamilton was slow in responding, local leaders throughout the state used a provision of the Provincial Government in order to muster their own militias. A Reverend John Elder, pastor of the Paxton Presbyterian Church of Paxtang mustered such a group of rangers. From the congregations of his church and a related one in Hanover, he managed to amass over 200 men who decided to take matters into their own hands. Today, we would call these men vigilantes, but at that time they were seen as "...truly the terror of the red men, swift on foot, excellent horsemen, good shots, skillful in pursuit or in escape, dexterous as scouts, and expert in maneuvering." Indeed, these men were very good at what they did, and what they did was kill Indians. They were indiscriminate in their choice of victim. A Christian or converted Indian died just as nicely as any other savage.

Throughout the fall of 1763 there had been various skirmishes between the whites and the natives. When whites burned Indian villages or killed Indians, they called it just recompense for savage brutality and told horror stories of whites who had died brutally at the hands of the Indians in various settlements and on several farms. The stories were true enough, but these "massacres" were often in retaliation for similar acts that had occurred against Indians.

The Paxtang Boys, as Rev. Elder's Rangers were commonly called, were out for blood that fall and they wanted the blood of an Indian named "Captain Bull" in particular. He was responsible for several killings in the Berks County area. Some of "Captain Bull's" Indians were supposedly traced to the village of Conestoga and others to the Moravian Indian missions at Main and Wichetunk.

When Rev. Elder's demand that all Indians be immediately removed from the area was denied, he and his men were outraged. They would have justice, and they particularly wanted the death of "Captain Bull" and all who had helped him.

All of this finally came to the ears of the new governor, John Penn who wrote, "The Indians of Conestoga have been misrepresented as innocent, helpless and dependent on this Government for support. The faith of this Government is pledged for their protection. I cannot remove them without adequate cause."

With those words the fate of the Conestoga was sealed.

At dawn on a cold December morning, the Paxtang Boys rode into the sleeping, and hitherto peaceful village of Conestoga where a group of Susquehannock Indians lived. Barking dogs were the only alert the natives had of the approach of the armed men. When the Conestoga looked out and saw what was upon them, they ran from their homes with tomahawks raised and this was then the excuse used to annihilate the ruthless savages bent upon making war!

"In a few minutes, every Indian fell before the unerring fire of the brave frontiersmen. Unfortunately, a number of Indians were absent from Conestoga..." So reports a contemporary account.

The truth of the attack is much more brutal than those few words indicate. The Indians were beaten, shot, and hacked apart. Women, children and even infants were not spared. One man would later write that among the rangers there were those who wasted not bullets upon the children. It has been said that they shattered the skull of a small boy. Along with that child, two women and three old men were killed. Fourteen Susquehannocks escaped and ran for cover. It was a cold, brutal trip. There was already several feet of snow upon the ground and these people had only the clothing they had on when the attack came.

The remaining Indians were quickly rushed into hiding. Some were sent to Philadelphia and hidden with Moravians there. Others were sent to Lancaster to the workhouse or prison where they were hidden in the jail. It was the hope of the Moravians who enlisted the aid of the jailer, that prison walls would protect the remaining Conestogas until word could come from Governor Penn that might offer them protection. Meanwhile, "Captain Bull" a couple old men and some women and small children were to be kept locked behind bars for their own protection.

When word reached the Paxtang Boys that their job was incomplete, they were furious. A Captain Steward of the Paxtang Boys whipped the men up and demanded that they ride to Lancaster and remove "Captain Bull" and take him to Carlisle Jail for trial. Fifty men rallied behind their captain and rode with him into Lancaster. They broke into the jail (later it would come out that the jailer had laid the keys on the desk and left the building unlocked by design) and rushed inside. Instead of finding these Conestogas willing to surrender, the few remaining people fought back as best they could. How could they do otherwise having heard what had befallen their village? This token resistance infuriated the Rangers and they began to beat, slash and hack apart the remaining Conestogas. Later, some of the men would describe the event and talk of women who threw themselves across their children and begged that their babies at least be spared. They spoke of breaking open children's heads with gun butts and smashing in the skulls of women who rocked dead babies and screamed. It was a horrible night's work.

The Lancaster Jail was torn down to build the Fulton County Opera House in 1852. However, the old entrance to the jail and some of the timbering still exists and the basement of the Opera House has a couple storage areas that had been part of the old jail. The impressions of what had happened there in 1763 seem to linger still.

When we arrived at the Fulton County Opera House, it was late at night and the director, Carl Hartman let us in. He is a debonair man with a soft voice and a passion for both the theater and the Fulton Opera House that became immediately evident. He knew that

we were there for ghost stories, though, so he started his tour in the foyer and gave us a brief history of the building.

As we talked, he led us down a hall, and then down a long ramp into the bowels of the theater.

"Last summer we had a family come for a visit by the name of Silverchain," began the director. "Mr. Silverchain was a Native American. He came with his wife and daughter. I tried to take them on a tour of the building, but very shortly it became obvious to me that they were not interested in the history of the theater. I asked them why they had come and they told me it was because of the Conestoga massacre."

Mr. Hartman took the family down the ramp into the basement. "Mr. Silverchain stopped me here, and said, 'this is the old building.'

Courtesy of The Fulton Opera House

There is no way to tell because of the wall design and I was thinking 'how did he know?'" The director led the family lower until they were in the large room where the remaining part of the prison can be seen. The director explained that Mr. Silverchain seemed very emotional. He walked over and stood quietly for a long while before a small plaque that was placed in the theater in 1997 to commemorate the death of the Conestoga.

"Finally Mr. Silverchain spoke," explained the director. "He touched the plaque--one name and said, 'that was my great, great, great grandmother. This boy was my great, great uncle.'"

Mr. Hartman could only stare at him for a second. He, like most folks thought that all of the Conestoga people were dead. Historically speaking they are, but there before him stood a last living link to those long ago people. Mr. Silverchain explained that his great, great, great grandmother had split up the two boys. One she kept with her in Lancaster and the other she sent with a family member on to Philadelphia. When the Paxtang Boys were turned back from Philadelphia, this remaining child was allowed to live. It was from this line that he traced his family.

Mr. Silverchain looked directly at a light colored stone in the wall. "You see that stone right there. I knew that this stone would be here. When I was a young man, I had a dream that there used to be stairs coming down to this space. I would fall down the stair-way every night in my dreams. I'd land on my feet and stare at that stone. I knew that stone would be there." The tone of Mr. Hartman's voice as he related Mr. Silverchain's words let us know how deeply he had been moved by the entire event.

With that, Mr. Silverchain shifted his gaze to a heavy wooden beam across the top of the gate. He laid his hand gently upon it. "This was here at that time, but not in this place." He spoke with such conviction that Mr. Hartman was convinced. What the man said made sense. Surely, when building the opera house, the architect used whatever good pieces he could salvage from the old prison to cut costs.

Again, Mr. Silverchain's gaze shifted as he looked around the room. "You know I can feel them down here...their presence. I'm not talking about ghosts; I mean their life ener-gy."

At this point Mrs. Silverchain spoke up. "Yes, I feel it in here, but I felt it much more strongly in that hallway just before we turned the corner."

Mr. Hartman just looked at Mrs. Silverchain. How could she know that at that turn they were closest to some of the secret places in the story of the death of the Conestoga?

Mr. Hartman told us that, by now, he was so convinced of the validity of this experi-ence that "I was willing to take them where they wanted to go."

"I led them to the orchestra pit, but Mr. Silverchain just shook his head and said 'No, I don't feel it in here.'"

Mr. Hartman told them that he could take them back under the theater and the fami-ly agreed that it was where they wanted to go.

Mr. Hartman led them through a maze of halls and rooms until they came to a small door. He took them into a room with a dirt floor and dirt piled up on both sides. It had been part of the original structure of the jail. He was now anxious to hear what Mr. Silverchain had to say.

Mr. Silverchain shook his head. "I feel a choking sensation in here, but this is not it." Mr. Hartman knew by now that the Indian wanted to go to the spot where his ancestors had died. He watched as Mr. Silverchain ran his hands through the dirt slowly, almost lov-ingly. He had the strong impression that if the Indian man had not been dressed up, he would have crawled through that dirt looking for links to his past.

"At this point I had an argument with myself because the next room, the old Green Room, is a store room now and I never let people in there, but I thought 'why not?'"

Mr. Silverchain stepped into that room and nodded. "They died here."

"You know," Mr. Hartman turned to look at us, "of all the places where there have been sightings of the ghosts, we have never had any down here. The ghosts here are all associated with the theater."

As Mr. Hartman told the story, he had been leading us through the various rooms in the basement and stopping where he had stopped with Mr. Silverchain and his family and relating what had transpired. I was quiet as I listened and watched. In the hallway where Mrs. Silverchain had indicated feeling a strong pull of life energy, Al's wife Jo had felt something, too. This was significant to me because Jo, by her own admission, never feels much in haunted places and rarely volunteers information of this sort, yet here she seemed almost compelled to explain her feelings.

As we walked back into the dirt room, I felt myself growing more agitated, but I thought it was because I knew what had transpired down here. I tried not to react. Al, though, was feeling something and began snapping photos. He would end up with a series of orb shots.

As we entered the old Green Room, Becky seemed to loose her breath. She felt odd and refused to take any photos. Her husband shot a couple and got an interesting shot. Becky seemed to feel it was disrespectful to take any photos where such misery was suffered. I can only applaud her compassion.

While we stood in that little room that had housed so many actors in the past, I could not help wondering about those who had died there before. Mr. Hartman and I began to talk about the story of the Conestoga. He explained that though the jailer had not actively participated in the massacre he had knowingly helped. He had arranged to leave the keys on the desk and went home knowing what would happen. "He didn't actively participate, but he certainly allowed them to do what they wanted to do," Mr. Hartman explained.

There was a moment of general silence as we all looked around. The echoes of the past rang in my ears and I felt dizzy there. I tried not to let it show, but I could hear those long ago cries.

With that, we left the history of the Conestoga behind and began our trek back up to the theater. Mr. Hartman related bits of history and tidbits of information as we went.

"You know, I have always wanted to see a ghost here, but I still haven't seen one. I keep trying." He turned and looked up at the balconies.

"You know I used to run the lights up on second balcony and the lady who ran them before me told me an interesting story. One night while she was working, an older African-American man came in and quietly sat down to watch the play. Now Second Balcony was closed at this time because they did not think it was strong enough to hold a full house. We ran lighting there before the last renovation and quite often members of the cast would have family or friends go up there to sit and watch the play. This woman did not think anything about this man because there was an African-American in the cast, so she just assumed that he was a relative.

"At the end of the play she turned to say something to the man about how he liked the performance, but there was no one there. She thought this was very odd because she should have seen and heard him leave, but she had not.

"She went down to the Green Room and found the African-American actor and asked him if he had a family member there that night. The man said not that he was aware of and asked her to describe the man she had seen. When she was done, the cast member looked at her oddly and smiled. 'Yes,' he said, 'That was my father, but he's been dead for ten years.'"

With that little tale our official ghost tour began.

We walked up on stage and carefully began to look around. Mr. Hartman explained that through the years there are two women who have been associated with this area. He pointed up. "Up there in the grid, I have been told, there is a woman who stays up there. I don't know much about her except to say that a man I knew who worked up on the grid saw her several times. By the way, that is the only wooden grid left in the United States." The pride and love for this building was coming through loud and clear in Mr. Hartman's voice, and I was rapidly growing to understand why.

"Over here," he indicated the far side of the stage. "Before we did the renovation, there was a stairway that went down to the lower level and there was a woman who sort of stayed in that area and went up and down that stairwell."

"One night we were working here about 3 o'clock in the morning striking set and I said to the other man, 'I really want to see a ghost here.' A few minutes later he said, 'Carl, turn around.' I turned and he said 'You just missed her. She just went down those stairs!' I keep trying, but maybe some of us aren't meant to see the ghosts."

Mr. Hartman went on to tell us of an account of the theater he had read that was written in the 1960's. This article related that at that time, several cast members had seen a hazy shape in the center isle (since removed during a renovation) while other actors on stage at the same time saw nothing.

"Originally, this theater was built as a flat floor no stage movie hall--that's why it was called an opera house--opera in the sense of vaudeville, not classic opera. There are some interesting stories here. In about 1870, an actress of national stature was here reciting when something happened that changed the course of this building. At that time, there was a business that distributed fertilizer to farmers in the lower level and the third floor was a men's club complete with shooting gallery and saloon. The smells must have been awful and that night, while this famous actress was reciting, something dripped down on her from above--we hope it was beer. Anyhow, she stopped and shouted, 'This is no fit place to perform.' She left the stage and the owner agreed with her. He shut the building down for 4 months and when he reopened, it was much like it is today. Of course, we've had another renovation recently, but still much of what was built back then is still here.

"Anyone who was anyone prior to 1940 played here. Mark Twain and Fredrick Douglas lectured here. Most of the Barrymores and Booths--not John Wilkes--played here. Buffalo Bill and Wild Bill Hickok and his Wild West Show played here. Now I've never seen it because it was plastered over before I came, but they tell me that there is a bullet hole up there from where Annie Oakley shot her gun. Sarah Bernhardt and John Phillip Sousa also were here and many more.

"In about 1930, the Fulton became a movie house. In 1960, it almost was torn down, but a group of citizens saved it. Oh, and the Movie *Witness* was filmed here and debuted in this theater."

I had assumed that this was the end of the ghost stories as we wandered the third floor and up into the offices. However, after treating us to a bit more history, Mr. Hartman came back to the topic for one last story.

"You know, back in 1997 when they put that plaque downstairs to commemorate the Conestoga, a group of Native Americans got together down on Water Street and had a ceremony. They burned braided sweet grass and afterward, our playwright-in-residence picked up a braid and brought it back. He took it to his office, which does not have an uncluttered inch. He's a wonderful man and very talented, but not very organized and anyhow he just laid the sweet grass braid on the bookcase inside the door, locked the room and left for the weekend. When he came back on Monday and unlocked the room, there was a clear path between the sweet grass and the window across the room. I mean there was nothing there. It was swept clear. No paper, nothing. I told Mr. Silverchain that and he just smiled and said, 'I can understand that.'"

As we thanked our host and left the building, I could not help but wonder exactly who we may have left behind. Were there Conestoga people there who are still not where they belong? Are there actresses or actors who did not succeed or who came back to tread the boards? Who could tell what might have been in that old building?

A year before, Rick Fisher and the Pennsylvania Ghost Hunter Society had set up shop in the building one night for a local television production. They had picked up orbs in the auditorium and their motion detectors had gone off when there was no visible reason. Mr. Hartman also told us that they picked up orbs on the one staircase. Who could that have been?

We left a lot of mysteries behind us at the Fulton Opera House that night. I can only hope to go back to enjoy a play some evening and perhaps to see a ghost while I'm there. And if you find yourself in the Lancaster area, I recommend stopping to see whatever is playing and to take the tour of the building. It will be an event you will never forget.

The Fulton Opera House charges a small fee for the tours, but they are worth it. To reach the Fulton Opera House Box Office for ticket information phone (717) 394-7133

OF REVENGE AND FORGIVENESS

In the previous story, I told you about the massacre of the Conestoga Indians at the old Lancaster jail and of the life energy from those long past people that is still there. However, there is much more to this story. The Paxtang Boys rode to Philadelphia in order to kill the last few Conestogas, but were met at the city limits by a group of citizens that included Benjamin Franklin. The citizens of Philadelphia were armed and refused to allow the mob past. The residents feared that the Paxtang mob would not be content to kill the Indians, but that they would burn the town or cause other trouble. The Quakers in Philadelphia had been speaking out against the murders and this also helped to move the citizens to action.

Governor John Penn was furious when he heard of the massacre and issued warrants for the scalps of Rev. Elder and several others for murder. In order to avoid loosing their lives, Elder and four others fled to the frontiers and hid for several years. During this time, friends of the Paxtang Boys persuaded Governor Penn to rescind the warrants against the men. Thus, there was no justice for the murdered innocents. But if a story related by Rev. Elder and written about by storyteller Mr. Henry Shoemaker from Altoona is true, a different lesson was learned by the man who led the vigilantes as they committed the cold-blooded murders.

Reverend John Elder had changed his name to Simon Rostraver during the years when he was being hunted for his part in the slaying of the Susquehannock Indians from the village of Conestoga in 1763. After the warrant for his scalp had been withdrawn, he had kept his new name and had returned to his first passion, the ministry. As an old man, he pastored the Slaney Church in Farmersmith not far from Letterkenny.

Through the years, he had often told stories from his life. Though he kept his new name, the pastor was proud to let everyone know that he had started life as Rev. John Elder, the fighting pastor. Like all old men, he loved to tell tales from his youth to his grandchildren and great-grandchildren and Rostraver's family well knew the story of the Paxtang Gang. Rostraver enjoyed painting himself as a great Indian hunter. In truth, he had the distinction of killing the last chief of the Conestoga band of the Susquehannocks, Captain Bull.

By now Rostraver/Elder was a very old man, but he had led a good life and he was satisfied. He was revered in his family and was cared for by a widowed daughter and his housekeeper. However, each winter his daughter would go visit her own children and grandchildren and another relative would come keep him company. This particular year his favorite great-granddaughter, Jodi had come to stay. He was not sure what he liked most about her; she was beautiful with blond curls and laughing eyes. She was sixteen and had the energy of youth that made him laugh, but most of all there was this intangible connection between the two despite the many years that they spanned.

One evening Jodi was invited to a sleighing party in Horse Valley. The young people were sleighing to a local pond where they would build big bonfires and wile away the cold night skating upon the frozen waters. Jodi was excited when she left looking as soft and pretty as a kitten in her cloak and fur muff.

Hours later, frantic knocks upon Rostraver's door called him up from drowsy reveries and he was rather glad for that evening his mind seemed bent upon remembering those long ago days when he had been hunting and killing the Conestoga people. At the door were several people from the skating party and they had with them Jodi. She had slipped and fallen into one of the bonfires and was badly burned. The poor girl was terrible to look at and in great pain. Terrified at what had happened to this favored grandchild, Rostraver led the men who carried Jodi to a big bedroom with the yellow walnut bedstead. Rostraver called for his housekeeper who bustled about caring for the child.

Rostraver knew that he had to get Jodi's mother and grandmother to the house quickly, but with the bad weather and heavy snow it would take hours. He imposed upon some of the men to send for the girl's family and returned to her.

By now, the housekeeper had cut away the burned clothing and rubbed the girl's burnt body with salve. The girl's face had fortunately been spared and with the blankets pulled up to her chin, Jodi would have looked lovely if not for the deathly pallor of her skin. The girl seemed to doze or loose consciousness and Rostraver was glad for that as he took up his seat beside the bed. His would be a long and terrible vigil. He sent the housekeeper to bed so she would be rested until she might be needed. He would watch Jodi. He could not sleep with her laying there looking like she would slip from this realm at any moment.

The wind whispered to the old man as he gazed at the fireplace. Fire, that which warmed and was so good, had this night done such harm. He shifted his eyes to the mantle where were carved the Gaelic words, "Far'm beil na laoich a dh'-fhalbh o shean, An cadal trom gun dol le ceol." The words were yet another memory from his past. This night was full of memories.

Beside the bed a single lamp was lit, and that pale flame and the fire in the grate were all that was needed for him to see by. He would sit up and speak soft, soothing words to Jodi when she would seem restless, and sit back thinking his own dark thoughts when she was quiet. He found the warmth of the room and the tension too much for an old man and he fell asleep.

In his dreams, he was the young John Elder once more. He was riding with the Paxtang Boys. He was in the Lancaster Work House Jail and he could hear the cries of the children. He remembered now the half-broken English of the women who begged not for their own lives, but rather that their children to be spared. He saw them as they fell before the rifle butts and heard the crunch of broken skulls as clubs struck the fatal blows. He remembered the eyes of the only man in the jail able to defend the women and children. It was Tenessedaga, "Captain Bull." This was the man they had come to get. He remembered how the man had looked. Tenessedaga had been a Canoy, a relative of the Susquehannocks, and now the old man remembered that last fight. It was not much of a battle for Rostraver had been armed and Tenessedaga had not been. Rostraver remembered how good it felt to pull that gun and shoot that cursed Indian. It was an act that he had lived his entire life being proud of.

Something woke the old man and he checked Jodi, but it was not her. Thankfully, the girl slept on. The clang of the clock perhaps?

The sound was of footsteps in the hall, but whose? His eyes sought the mantle clock and he knew that there was no way Jodi's family could have arrived yet. There in the doorway, the old man's eyes strained to see the movement. It was Tenessedaga in his full chief robes. The Indian stood looking at him while leaning on a long rifle. Insane! Though he was of Gaelic ancestry, Rostraver did not believe in ghosts. He blinked his eyes and rubbed them, but still Tenessedaga remained and the old hatred swelled in the old man's breast.

Had this Indian come now to take his Jodi? Rostraver stood and glared at the Indian. He demanded what the Indian wanted and banished him from the house. He made threats to kill the Indian, but he knew they did no good--for he had killed this man many years ago.

Through it all, the Indian just smiled at him without rancor. Why was he so pleased with himself, the old man thought franticly?

Jodi's voice shook the old man when she spoke. "Grandpa, what does that Indian mean?" The girl grabbed at her grandfather.

Now Rostraver was even more furious, but Tenessedaga did not seem perturbed at all. The old man dashed sideways and grabbed up a chunk of wood that he tossed at the Indian. The wood passed right through without harm. Still smiling, Tenessedaga turned and started down the hall toward the attic stairs. On the way, he passed the housekeeper who had been alerted to trouble by the voices. She gasped when she saw the Indian. She ran into the girl's room while Rostraver gave chase.

The attic was empty, though there was nowhere for the Indian to go. Rostraver searched until the clock chimed one a.m. When he returned to Jodi, she was anxious, excited. "Was he a ghost, Grandpa? Was he the chief you killed? What does he want?"

He did not answer for he greatly feared what that answer would truly be.

In his mind, he heard the screams of those long dead women and children as they were beaten to death by clubs and rifle butts. He remembered the sounds, the smells, and the sight of the blood. Tenessedaga had surely come for revenge. Revenge was what had killed him and now revenge would take Jodi.

Suddenly, there were excited voices downstairs and in seconds Jodi's mother and grandmother were in the room. After allowing the women to assure themselves of Jodi's condition, Rostraver demanded to know how they had gotten there so soon. He had reckoned that it would be daylight before they would arrive.

His daughter and granddaughter both told him a similar story of awaking to the sight of an Indian man who had told them that Jodi was badly hurt and that they must hurry to her. With such a vision, the two women had little doubt that something drastic had happened. They had been in their carriage and well on the way before anyone had come for them. The old Indian had frightened them terribly.

Through bloodless lips Rostraver admitted that the Indian had been there, too, and he told them the man's name. They well knew name from the stories of old.

Suddenly, Rostraver's shoulders slumped. He had expected revenge from his old enemy, but instead the Indian had offered him forgiveness. Sixty years ago, Rostraver as John Elder had taken Tenessedaga's life in a heinous manner, and now, in return for that act, he had been shown mercy by his victim. His heart was moved by the fact that even Indians must enter Heaven, and Indians, whom he had long called savages, knew how to show mercy where revenge was due.

Jodi recovered and Rostraver would begin a new chapter in his life. He replaced his pride with shame for the murders he had committed and he carried forever after the certain knowledge that the greatest act of kindness ever committed on his behalf had been committed by a dead Indian.

GETTYSBURG TOURISTS' TALES

(Gettysburg, Adams County)

I have been invited by author Mark Nesbitt, (who writes the Ghosts of Gettysburg books) to book signings throughout the past two years. In that time, I have come across several interesting stories from tourists who came to the Ghost Tours to meet us. Of course, I can not verify these stories or promise you that they are true. I can only tell you that these stories were told to me as true by some very rattled people.

By far the most common reports coming in from the battlefield in Gettysburg are about sounds and smells. One evening a couple came in to the Ghost Tours and told me that they had just come from the battlefield. The gentleman was very interested in the history of the area and in guns. He insisted that while they were on the battlefield near Little Round Top they had heard guns of Civil War vintage going off. Now the man was quite adamant that he collected guns and knew that different ones made different sounds. He furthermore, insisted that the style of gun used during the Civil War was one of his favorites to collect and he had several that he often shot. The couple looked around for re-enactors while on the perch atop Little Round Top, but saw no one. They determined that the sounds were coming from around a curve that they could not see around. The shots sounded several more times while they were there. They decided to walk down to see the re-enactors.

As the couple hurried in that direction, they continued to hear the sounds. Now they were near Plum Run where fierce fighting had occurred. The couple rounded the curve and there was sudden silence, but the smell of gunpowder was strong. This area is actually a small field and there was nowhere for the re-enactors to go in such a hurry.

I listened to the couple's story as they vehemently avowed what had just happened to them. I believed that they thought they had experienced something odd, but was it possible that it was a trick?

About an hour went by while I signed books and chatted to patrons. At length another family came my way. They were interested in the ghost stories and we chatted a bit as they browsed through my book. Finally the teenaged girl seemed about to explode. "Tell her, Daddy," she insisted. "I'll bet she'll believe us."

The girl's father seemed embarrassed by his daughter's outburst, but he gave his wife a look and she was nodding encouragement, too. These folks obviously had a story to tell.

"Well I'm not at all sure I believe in this stuff," the man began, as his face reddened slightly. "But a while ago, oh about an hour or a little more, we were walking around the battlefield just looking around when we heard shooting. We were at Devil's Den going over those rocks and heard guns going off. The smell of powder came to us on a little breeze and we thought there was a re-enactment going on. We decided to walk through the woods to the spot where the sounds were coming from. It only took us a few minutes to get there, but when we arrived there was no one around. Now the smell of powder was really strong, and there was something else while we looked around. We could smell, I guess it was pipe smoke but it was really sweet. We did not see anyone." The man shrugged as if he was at a loss for words.

I could not help wanting to know more. "Do you have any idea where you were when this happened?" I queried. The mother and daughter shook their heads, but the girl piped up. "We were near a little stream."

Her father glanced at me and muttered. "I think they call that Plum Run or something..."

I recalled that first couple about an hour earlier who had a very similar experience at the same location. Were there re-enactors there? Not one person all evening came in talking about any, but at least three other couples did mention hearing gun shots near Plum Run.

Stories like this one have come in several times. People talk of hearing gun shots, of smelling gun smoke, of smelling pipe smoke, or of seeing a fleeting figure who suddenly disappears. Many folks have experienced seeing a hobo-like man who is barefoot and shabbily dressed. The fellow has long hair and a beard and is seen around Little Round Top. He is believed to be the ghost of a Texas soldier who fought and died there. The soldiers from Texas were a rag-tag bunch by the time the arrived at Gettysburg. Their shoes were mostly gone, their clothes rags. They were far from home and their care packages, if they had any, rarely reached them. Many of them looked like hobos.

Occasionally, a person will come from Little Round Top with a story of seeing a mysterious, bare-foot hobo who seems to just disappear as he walks along the area.

Perhaps one of the most dramatic sightings I have ever personally heard of came in July of 2000. It was the Fourth of July weekend and I was, once again, signing books at the Ghost Tours of Gettysburg. There were long lines of folks to meet Mark and I. A young blond woman seemed to be hanging back. Her fair complexion was red and her eyes were tearing. Her hands were shaking and she was twisting a tissue between her fingers, shredding it. I thought that this young woman was going to cry. A couple times, she switched lines as if unsure of who to approach first. She then hung back again and waited until the crowd thinned. When I had the opportunity, I pointed her out to Mark who was likewise concerned. He could see the young woman appeared distressed. At last, she approached us and her appearance was one of a person in shock.

The woman broached the subject carefully for a few seconds. She asked if we had ever had any experiences around Devil's Den? Mark told her a couple stories and offered her some water. Slowly, the woman began to calm down. A young man joined her and she began to gain control. She indicated the man and introduced him as her husband. They had only been married a few months. The husband began to tell us an incredible story about being at Devil's Den that day. As he spoke, the young woman once more grew agitated and tears slid down her face. She interrupted her husband to correct the story.

"We decided to drive down here for today because it's the anniversary of the battle and all and *Jon," she indicated her husband, "is really fascinated by the history here." The woman was shaking again. Her fingers endless working that hankie and that image stuck with me. When I was twelve and my sister seven, our father died. At the viewing, my little sister did the very same thing to release her terrible stress. This was body language that spoke volumes to me about this woman's emotional state.

"I didn't want to come down, but I agreed. We were out at Devil's Den when I decided that I was getting tired and wanted to go back to the car. Jon was up on the boulders and I told him where I was going. He said okay, and stayed there. There were other tourists climbing over the rocks, too. So, I walked down across the field and just as I was about to cross the road a young soldier came out of the woods down below. I thought he was a re-enactor who was in character. He seemed surprised and pleased that I could see him. He had a southern accent and said that his name was Timmy Wells or Walls, I couldn't tell which because of the accent, but I think he meant Wells. He told me that he had come from Tennessee with his infantry unit. They had all been killed elsewhere and pointed off vaguely. He told me that he had joined the Texans and was fighting with them here. Then the young man looked very sad, there was dirt on his face and his hair was matted down. He said, "Ma'am could ya' tell 'em that I just wanna go home now? I wanna see my mama, could ya tell 'em, please?"

At this point, the young woman was quite impressed with this young soldier and his tale. She thought that the re-enactor should have been a full-time actor and she was going to tell him that he was really very good. Suddenly, another man, older, and with dark hair and a beard, stepped out of the woods. He yelled, "Timmy, Timmy, time to go now." The young man with his dirty blond hair turned back to the young woman. "I gotta go now," he said in that slow southern drawl. He reached down and plucked a plastic flower from one of the wreaths that had been left in memory of those who had died so long ago. He handed the flower to her and smiled softly. "You've been a peach of a belle, Ma'am. "With that, he turned toward the darker man. As he walked back toward the woods, both men in gray began to fade away. Suddenly, the young woman realized that she had not just witnessed a re-enactor, but she had just experienced something else. "I still have the flower in my pocket; do you want to see it?"

As the young woman ended her story, her husband jumped in. "You know I don't like this stuff much, but I saw the whole thing. The whole group of tourists on the rocks with me saw it, too. After the men faded out, they started talking, whispering, and then some of them shouted. They were excited and upset about this whole thing.

The young woman seemed relieved when her story was over. Once again, she asserted that she should not have come to Gettysburg. Why not, we wanted to know?

She glanced at her husband and he nodded. "I've never had stuff like this happen before. No, that's not true. There was an event when I was a kid and we were at a dude ranch. I kept talking about an old cowboy that no one else saw, but I saw him really clearly. I used to hear an old woman talking in a house we lived in when I was about 14, but she didn't scare me. But that was years ago. We got married in February of this year and we spent our honeymoon at the James Getty Hotel. Our first night there, I awoke to see a man standing by the bed looking at us. He just faded away. Well, I took a towel from the hotel as a souvenir of our honeymoon. I had to throw it away because I'd see the same man at our house. He'd be standing there watching me sleep and stuff. It really freaked me out. Now this..."

When the couple had finally calmed down, given us their e-mail address and phone number and left, Mark turned to me. "A lot of people don't know it, but the Texans did fight in that area." That was all he said.

I later contacted a group that does research on the Civil War and asked them if they could tell me if there was a Timmy or Timothy Wells who served in the Civil War from Tennessee. The reply offered me five possibilities.

"Wells, T. B. Private, "A" Company 5th Cavalry
Wells, T. J., Private "D" Company, 8th Infantry
Wells, T. P., "G" Company, 18th Infantry
Wells, T. W., Private, "F" Company, 14th Consolidated Calvary
Wells, T. W., Private, "G" Company, 4th Infantry"

If we eliminate the cavalrymen, that allows us three privates, anyone of whom could have been the mysterious Timmy who is still longing to go home.

I spoke to the young couple several times after that night. The young woman was suddenly inundated by psychic impressions and it seemed to be overwhelming her. She insisted that she avoided the Triangular Field because of the great pull it held for her. She had visited it once before the psychic visions began. Now, she greatly feared that if she returned to the area, she would see bloody bodies and hear the cries of the dead.

Of course, I've heard many other tales of ghostly goings on. A visit to Spangler's Spring one evening brought me several tales. While walking around, I overheard a family saying, "Now this is where we saw her." I listened as they told the story of a previous visit during which they had seen a woman who seemed to glow slightly moving away from the spring into the woods in the distance.

I waited for a pause in the conversation and introduced myself. Before long, I was being inundated by stories from regular weekenders at Gettysburg. Many came for the military history, but just as many had come for the haunted history as well. I met a fellow named Chet who was destined to become a friend. Through him, I met others who had stories to tell. It seems that an entire subculture of weekend ghost hunters come to Gettysburg and have created for themselves a loose network. They wander the battlefields usually being sure to visit two spots. Just before the park closes, they make it to Spangler's Spring, and after the park closes, they go to Sach's Bridge. They cause no harm and just wander around talking or looking at the site. There has been no damage or any reason why they shouldn't be there. It is a touchstone in their lives and a place where any given Saturday night I know I can find Chet.

From Chet and his network of weekenders comes the next group of stories. Chet has had several experiences during his time in Gettysburg. Of course, if Gettysburg is as haunted, as many believe, it would make sense that he'd have had several experiences, as he's there just about every weekend.

Spangler's Spring seems to be quite active and Chet has reported that one evening when he was walking along a path from the main area to what he calls the "outhouse" he got slightly separated from the group he was with. He was not particularly upset about this development as he has tramped most of Gettysburg and knew exactly where he was and where he was going. Suddenly, he heard the thud of heavy footfalls and labored breathing coming rapidly up behind him. Turning toward the sound, he realized that no one was on the path behind him. Quickly, he snapped a photo and ran to catch the group.

On another night, Chet said that while walking along Spangler's Spring with some friends, they found themselves upon the same path. He suddenly felt something strike him on the back of the head, and it hit hard enough to knock his hat off. He whirled around to see who was pulling a prank, but no one was behind him.

Another person confided to me that they return to Spangler's Spring as often as they can because they saw the White Lady said to haunt this area. She and her husband are hoping to see her once more, and this time they are armed with a video camera. Another couple claims to have already video taped the White Woman, but, though the couple promised me the video, I have not seen it yet.

Yet another couple returns because of an experience that their adult daughters had there one evening. One of the young women had her long hair pulled back into a ponytail while the other girl wore her hair loose and long. As the family hiked the area on that evening, the girl with the ponytail suddenly cried out. When her sister turned back, she too, cried out. The first sister's ponytail was standing straight up in the air as if invisible hands held it upright. The girls were frightened and ran.

In October of 2000, a group of friends and I went to Gettysburg for an evening of wandering the battlefield. We had a great time and had a few interesting experiences. However, the most interesting one was not discovered until long after that night. One of the group members named Annette had been running a cassette player on the battlefield. Annette later told me that she found a voice calling out "Get me!" over and over at the Devil's Den while we were talking. I can honestly say that I was there that night and heard no such thing. Yet, it is very clear on that tape. Is there still a man lying among those rocks crying out eternally for help?

A second electronic voice phenomena (EVP) was discovered and this one sounds like the being of a speech. Again, no one was stumping for political office that night. However, at one time the tourist trade actually had brought a need for streetcars to transport the visitors to the battlefield. Such a track lays all but forgotten near Devil's Den to this day. Here political candidates used to stump for votes quite often. Apparently, one is still making his plea for election.

There are many more battlefield tales to be told about visitors who came for the history, but left with ghostly tales to tell. If you have had such an experience, please let me know and next time I might be adding your story to the growing list of tales of tourists at Gettysburg.

GRANDFATHER'S SPIRIT

(Altoona, Blair County)

Divorce is a terrible word for most children. Suddenly their world turns upside down and they loose one of their parents--usually their father. No matter what the reasons for divorce, children usually loose out. Statistics tell us that even today when parents split up; there is a dramatic drop in the woman's income and, therefore, a dramatic drop in the money to care for the children. This disparity was even more pronounced in the 1960's when Theresa's parents split up. Her mother had to move home, bringing Teresa and her sisters along. At least in Theresa's case, her grandparents had a large home in the Altoona area big enough to accommodate the family.

For Theresa, this time was mellowed by her grandparents whom she came to truly love. Her Grandpa George became a central figure, taking the place of her father in many ways. It was a close, loving relationship between Grandpa George and all of the girls, but in 1973 their world would once more be shattered. Grandpa George had a sudden, fatal heart attack. It was quick for him, but for the little girls the loss was extremely difficult. In fact, the entire household was devastated by this loss. Theresa was only eleven years old when Grandpa George passed away, and this was the first time she would be touched by death. It was a hard lesson to learn and was made especially hard, as Grandpa George had been a vigorous man who had not seemed ready to die.

Grandpap Grandma & Theresa Pike
photo courtesy of Theresa Pike

Theresa's impressions would be born out very shortly. Grandpa George *was not* ready to pass on; in fact, he had never left them.

Only a week after the funeral, Theresa was laying in her bed in the room she shared with her sisters, thinking about her Grandfather and trying to come to terms with the loss of this beloved man in her life. Suddenly she realized that she heard something in the room next door--Grandpa George's room. As she listened, she recognized the sound immediately. Grandpa George had an old metal bed with metal bedsprings within the frame. Whenever he would lie down, the springs would creak with his body weight. It was a familiar sound, but one she should not be hearing as no one went into Grandpa's room except Grandpa. Her Grandmother slept downstairs.

Theresa was frightened because she could not understand what her ears were hearing. She not sure what to do, but by the next night she had decided to tell her sisters what she had heard. The other girls all agreed that they would stay awake to see if it happened again. It did not take long before the distinctive sound of squeaking bedsprings was heard in Grandpa George's room. The other girls all agreed that it was the bedsprings in Grandpa's bed. Now Theresa had witnesses, but that really didn't help much. In the morning, the girls excitedly told their Grandma and mother about the sounds.

Far from chiding the children for their imagination, the adults seemed to believe them. However, their Grandma realized that the girls were frightened, so she took them aside and told them that if what they heard was Grandpa, then they should not be frightened. Grandpa George had loved them and never hurt them in life, so they should not fear him now. He still loved them and would never hurt them. Death did not change love, and Grandpa still loved them very much, Grandma said.

Buddy and Theresa Pike
photo courtesy of Theresa Pike

Grandma's soothing words helped all of the little girls cope with the nightly squeaking bedsprings. They would hear them each night, and though they still felt frightened a little, they believed Grandma and knew that Grandpa George would not hurt or frighten them.

One night, about two weeks after the bedsprings began squeaking at night, Theresa laid in the darkness waiting for the nightly squeaking to end. She lay in bed watching the doorway and trying to ignore the sound. At last it stopped, but she was suddenly surprised to see the glowing figure of Grandpa George walking down the hall. He walked just as he had in life; he had on his nightclothes and was smoking a cigarette just has he had done in life. She actually saw the glowing tip of the cigarette in the darkness and she knew that Grandpa was on his way down the hall to the bathroom just as he had done so often. The sight only lasted a few seconds, but it was enough for Theresa. She had no doubt that she had seen Grandpa George. In the morning, Theresa would learn that her sisters, too, had seen Grandpa George on his way down the hall that night.

Only a few nights after the girls had seen their grandfather, their mother was to have her own very special visit from Grandpa George. Their mom had been in bed sleeping when she suddenly felt a hand upon her shoulder shaking her gently and waking her up. She opened her eyes to see her father's glowing form in his pajamas looking at her. "There's a baby in trouble. Hurry, it needs help." The words formed in Theresa's mother's head, though her father had not spoken a word. As soon as he was sure that she understood the message, her father had faded away.

Theresa's mother got out of bed and hurried downstairs to where her mother was still working in the kitchen. She immediately told her mother the entire story of her father waking her and telling her that a baby was in trouble. At that time, the family had a cousin whose wife was pregnant and Theresa's mother thought that might be the baby her father had meant. However, suddenly her mother stopped. Her face changed as if something was dawning upon her, and she turned and hurried from the kitchen calling, "Just wait a minute."

Grandma hurried to the stairs and up the landing to where she could see into the house across the street from the landing window. There, Grandma saw the young woman who lived across the street on the telephone and crying. She was talking and pacing back and forth. In a rush, she hurried down the stairs and out the front door. Before Theresa's mother could stop her, the older woman was across the street knocking upon the door.

The young woman opened the door and quickly Grandma ascertained that her little baby was sick. The young woman had called the doctor who had told her to call him in the morning if the baby was still sick, but not to worry for the night. However, the young woman was very scared and she had been crying and talking to her own mother when Grandma had come over. Grandma took a look at the tiny baby and told that girl to get the child to the hospital immediately. The young woman seemed relieved to be doing something and quickly left.

The next day, the family was going their about normal business when the young woman from next door came to the house. She wanted to know how Grandma had known that her baby was deathly sick? Grandma told the whole story truthfully and simply. The young woman was amazed. She told them that the doctor in the emergency room had told her that if she had waited until morning the baby would have been dead. She could not believe what had happened to save her baby's life. Grandpa George had always loved children and he had not been able to stand by and let this little baby die. His intervention had saved the baby's life!

After that, they heard no more of Grandpa George. His bedsprings no longer squeaked, he did not walk the hallway, nor did he ever appear to anyone in the family. It seemed that Grandpa George had finally passed on. His last earthly deed had been enough, and now he had found peace. That was until early in the year 20000.

I received a letter from Theresa in September of 2000 that detailed her Grandfather's story. The amazing part I will let her tell you herself. She wrote:

"We didn't have any more experiences until my sister's son was around 5 years old...

"One afternoon, I received a frantic telephone call from my sister. She was upset. I told her to calm down and tell me what's wrong. She told me she was going past her son's room. She heard him talking to someone. She looked in on him and asked whom was he talking to? He answered, 'my friend.' She asked him, 'What Friend?'

He answered, 'My friend, George.'

Knowing George was our grandfather's name, she asked him what George looked like? Her son went on to describe a tall man with white hair and a bent finger. Grandpa George had a finger broken during an Indian wrestling match. It was never set, so it healed bent. My sister was absolutely sure now, her son was talking to his great grandfather. I told her, 'After what we saw, it shouldn't come as a surprise. He would want to see the great grandchildren he didn't see in life.'

It's been almost 28 years since his death. I am glad to know of an afterlife. I take comfort in knowing our loved ones never really leave."

I, too, take comfort from stories like Theresa's. It is wonderful to know that Grandpa George came back to visit yet another generation of his family. I am told that often dead relatives come back to visit the living. It somehow makes death less final when they may still return.

THE STONE HOUSE

(McKee, Blair County)

You, the reader, are often quite generous with your own stories. Whether you write them down for me, or you save them to tell me in person, I'm always pleasantly surprised by your wonderful tales. The story of the Stonehouse is a great example of how you are all responsible for stories coming to me. After telling stories at the Martinsburg, PA library, I was approached by two ladies who had some stories to tell. The one woman told me about a place nearby that she had long heard was haunted. I thanked her and decided to call the owners and ask if they knew of any haunted history for their business. The owner, Carol Fowler, was so generous with not only her time, but her information as well. Thus, I was able to learn about two very different ghosts who both inhabit the Stonehouse.

McKee is an anonymous little village with a main highway that bisects it. However, there was a time when the village of McKee was well known. It was well known because it was home to Martha's Furnace. Martha's Furnace was an iron ore furnace built by Edwin F. Shoenberger in 1844. E.F. Shoenberger would build several furnaces and forges. He would build Upper Maria Forge in 1828, Middle Maria Forge in 1830 and Lower Maria Forge in 1832, and all were located in McKee. Shoenberger also built forges and furnaces throughout Blair County, and many of these he also named after his daughters.

The Stone House was built as a storage building for supplies for Martha's furnace. However, it would soon come into other uses. From a storehouse, it evolved until the building flirted with fame as the headquarters of the McKee Gap Pennsylvania Emergency Militia of Minutemen in 1863.

The Civil War was raging into the north in 1863 and word spread through Pennsylvania that General Lee and his rebels were moving through the southern part of the state raiding as they went. It became clear to the people of Blair County that if Lee made it much further into the state he would try to take Altoona and topple the hub of northeastern rail transport. This would interrupt the supply lines of the north and give Lee an opportunity to put the enemy in a weakened and defensive position.

A group of men, either too old or ill for the military or too young to join up, mustered together and prepared a defense in case Lee did turn his troops toward Altoona. It was known that he'd probably take the Loysburg Gap, and then come straight up the valley, right through McKee. The McKee Militia prepared to stop Lee's troops in McKee.

The aim of these men was a high one, but locally people did not appreciate the men's efforts. They made jokes about the militia and belittled them. The militia became known locally as the "Chicken Raiders" because they were not given any rations and had to poach local poultry in order to feed themselves.

However, the ghosts of the Stonehouse Inn do not come from that part of history. These are not historic spirits in the usual sense. They come from the families who lived in the house and who died there.

The first spirit in the house is believed to be a woman named Naomi Burket who lived many years in the house. Mrs. Burket was a small woman. She was well loved in the community. After her death, the house was sold, but her family, along with Carol, believes that Naomi has remained behind. Carol has had guests talk about footsteps upon the stairs, about odd noises in the master bedroom, and one resident of the house spoke of hearing knocking downstairs and a sound she thought was knocking on the door or a door opening. Upon investigation, she found the house securely locked up.

Carol, however, believes that her first encounter with Naomi came when she walked into the downstairs parlor one day and found a rocking chair gently rocking by itself. She would later find out from a relative of Naomi's that the woman had often enjoyed sitting in that room rocking quietly.

The Stonehouse is now a bed-and-breakfast and restaurant. A couple years ago Carol hosted a wedding reception there. At the reception was a granddaughter of Naomi. The family throwing the party was serving wine. Later, Carol spoke to Naomi's granddaughter who surprised her. The young woman told her that Naomi had not been pleased about the wine imbibing going on in her home. She said she felt Naomi in a corner of the room shaking her head disapprovingly.

The second spirit is much more tragic in nature. A resident approximately 30 years ago had a teenage son who hung himself in the garage of the property. (I'll not give the family's name so as to spare them pain.) It was a terrible event for the family and they could not remain at the house, however their son seems to still be there.

In the early winter of 2001, Carol had a couple come spend a night in the Stonehouse. The next morning the couple greeted Carol with a question. "Do you know your bed-and-breakfast is haunted?"

Carol certainly did know about Naomi, but she asked them what they meant. The woman told her about a little woman who haunted the building, and then, she surprised Carol by saying, "and there's a young man here, too. He's a teenager and he killed himself here, but not in the house, it was in one of the out buildings. He just wants someone to know he's still here." The woman explained that she was sensitive to this type of phenomena and that she had dreamed about the two spirits. The woman's husband, a Native American, told Carol that he felt that this building was built over old Indian land. He felt their essence there.

His wife said, "Yes, I believe that there are layers upon layers of spirits here." She asked if they could go to the basement, but it was impossible because the stairs were cluttered and a bit dangerous.

After the couple left, Carol was telling her husband about this conversation and he reminded her of the walk he had uncovered the previous summer. It was a walk that went to nowhere. It very well could have belonged to an earlier building.

After hearing all of these stories, I was most anxious to bring the Central Pennsylvania Paranormal Association to the house for a meeting. Carol not only graciously hosted us, she also allowed us to tour the building while she gave us all of the information she knew about the property. Though it was very interesting, we did not encounter anything paranormal. We all enjoyed the house, but left feeling that we had missed something.

That all changed when a few days later a member of the group, Annette called to tell me that she had nine confirmed and two more possible EVP recordings from the Stonehouse. She explained that a young man had spoken after Scott Crownover had suggested that the batteries in Annette's camera were drained. This voice said, "Very." An older sounding woman then says, "Good." Later, on the second floor, Annette had another problem with the camera working and again Scott told her to check the batteries. This time the male voice says, "more batteries." (We have found that often batteries in our equipment will be drained when we are at haunted sites. It seems that these entities use the electrical energy in the batteries to help themselves manifest.)

On and on the two voices offer comments as the group walked around. Somehow, these spirits had managed to elude the other equipment, but they had allowed themselves to be recorded.

Whether you believe in ghosts or not, I highly recommend the Stonehouse as a place to dine and perhaps spend a night. Carol is a lovely woman who will charm you right away. And if you do happen to see a chair rocking by itself or hear footsteps on the stairs in the middle of the night when you are alone in the building, you must be sure to tell Carol and me.

THE TRAGIC DEATH OF
LILLIE WRIGHT SHOWALTER

(Breezewood, Bedford County)

From time to time, I meet people who tell me that their homes are haunted. Many of them have only vague feelings that something is amiss in their homes and they can't explain exactly why they believe their house is haunted. I often ask them if they have researched the history of the home and about 90 percent of them have not. With no real manifestations and with no history to work from, I can do little. Then I meet people like Mary. Mary is a vivacious, friendly woman in the prime of life who came to one of my lectures. She and her daughter insisted that Mary's house is haunted. During a lecture, I cannot stop and follow up, but Mary was thankfully not going to let the subject drop.

We began an organization called the Central Pennsylvania Paranormal Association (CPPA) to investigate hauntings and to help people who live in haunted houses. Living in a haunted house can be either a thrilling experience or it can be a terrible one. Either way, there are many folks who just need someone to listen to them so that they feel validated. They need to know that they are not alone with such experiences.

Mary came to the first meeting of the CPPA held in the Jean Bonnet Tavern (check out the chapter about the new phenomena at the Jean Bonnet). She came with two of their daughters and they brought photographs to support their story. I took one look at the pictures and knew that Mary was not exaggerating. She definitely did have a haunted house and a haunted yard, and a haunted field and an entire haunted property!

At the meeting, I found the time to talk to Mary and her daughters for a few minutes and they told me a fantastic tale. Mary is a woman who falls into that 10 percent who have researched their home's history. She knew exactly who and what was haunting her property.

First of all, former owners had told her that there had once been an Indian village on a nearby hill. When they had plowed the hill and turned it into a field, they had literally taken buckets full of Indian artifacts from the plowed earth.

Mary speculated that since her home sat below the field where the village had been, her yard might have been used as a Native American graveyard. She had read a bit on this subject and the books she had looked at described how a village would have been laid out and her yard was in the correct position to have been the likeliest sight chose by the natives for their burial ground.

The second piece of information about the haunting was of a much more recent vintage. One of the previous owners had been a woman named Lillie Wright Showalter. Lillie and her husband Orville had built the house that Mary now owned. Lillie had lost her husband to pneumonia in 1934. Lillie had been left with a twelve-year-old daughter, Dora and an eleven-year-old son, Elwin.

Lillie must have thought she was a very lucky woman when a local fellow named Glen Showalter began courting her. He asked her to marry him, and on April 4th, 1938 Lillie added Showalter to her name. But Lillie's marriage was not destined to be a happy one.

At first, Lillie must have been pleased that Glen wanted to spend time with her teenaged children, but soon she had to realize that Glen preferred to spend time with Dora, now sixteen-years-old and not fifteen-year-old Elwin. It was Dora whom he made trek along with him up Bill's Place Mountain to help him cut firewood. It was Dora whom he insisted upon helping in the summerhouse where they could be alone.

In little more than a year, Lillie's happiness was forever shattered. In August, Lillie's daughter confessed that she was pregnant and that the child belonged to Glen Showalter. Lillie was devastated. This was the ultimate betrayal on Glen's part, and she had to have had conflicted feelings about Dora at that moment, too. Was it possible that Dora had been a willing victim or was she forced to participate in Glen's evil schemes?

The stress was too much for Lillie and she had a nervous breakdown. Glen made sure that the neighbors knew of this.

Dora's condition could not be hidden forever and word got out that Dora was pregnant. Most folks did not believe Lillie when she told that that it was Glen's child, after all, had she not just had a mental breakdown?

According to Glen, he heard a shot around 4 p.m. on Sept. 2nd, 1939 and went to investigate. He found Lillie's body slumped on the steps of a small tool shed by the summerhouse. She had wrapped a curtain around a shotgun to hold it in place, and then used the rod to push the trigger. Lillie had committed suicide.

Dora and her tragic child would die later that year after a difficult birthing. Elwin would grow up without any family now.

Glen was forced to leave the property when it had to be sold to cover Lillie's debts. The best information I could find was that Glen had never remarried. He finally took ill and when he realized that he was dying he sent for a minister. On his deathbed, he confessed to murdering Lillie back in 1939 and to faking the suicide. He wanted to be forgiven so that he could go to Heaven.

With a history like that one, Mary certainly had a right to suspect that her house was haunted. She began to show me her photographs and explain where and when they were taken. Outside the summerhouse, where the shed had once stood, there were always many, many orbs that she could see on her digital camera. She had photographs of them taken on both a 35-mm and a digital camera. What had intrigued her ever since first capturing an orb was that these orbs were often seen in the area where the shed steps had once been. Could Lillie still be lingering where she had been placed after the murder?

Another place where they always captured many orbs was around the large satellite dish in her back yard. This area is close to where the Indian village had once stood, and here she often caught dozens of orbs in motion. Did they relate to that Indian village?

However, Mary has also caught orbs and ectoplasm on photographs all around her property. She showed me photographs with large red and yellow streaks all over them. She showed me photographs with dozens of orbs and photographs with red orbs on them.

In her home, Mary had noticed that her little dog would often suddenly sit up and stare intently at a spot as if someone had just come toward it. One day she decided to snap a picture when she saw this happen. This was the first photograph of ectoplasm in her home. Since then, she has caught it several

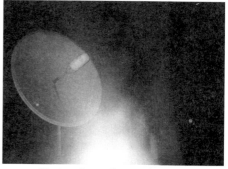

Eerie mist at former home of
Lillie Wright Showalter

other times and also has caught pictures of orbs moving through the house.

I asked Mary if she would mind if Becky and I visited her home. Mary was more than gracious about the invasion and on a partly clear night Becky and I showed up. Mary took us into the kitchen for coffee while we waited for darkness to fall. During the course of the evening, Mary revealed many details about the haunting. One of her daughters had recently been laying on a couch resting when she felt someone touch her shoulder. The young woman had quickly turned over, but no one else was there.

Mary told us about the fact that the dog and the cats often seem to be watching someone she can not see. She also told us that through the years there have been various mysterious incidents. One evening Mary noticed her dog sitting up watching something and

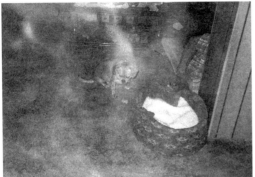

she decided to snap a photograph of it. When she saw the picture, Mary was surprised because in front of the dog there was a patch of mist--mist that she had not been able to see with the naked eye. She quickly assured us that she was not cooking and no one was smoking in her home when this mysterious photograph was taken.

Mary and her one daughter related that when the girls were teenagers, one of them had gotten home late from a date. She went to her room and heard footsteps. She thought her mother was checking on her when her bedroom door opened, but no one was there. Then, the closet swung open and that frightened the girl enough that she pulled up the blankets and did not look around until morning. Could it have been Lillie checking to be sure the girl was okay?

Photo of ectoplasm in Mary's home
photo by Mary Foor

One of the other daughters had heard footsteps on the stairs. The girls also had seen or heard the closet door opening at night several times.

However, one of the most unusual incidents that Mary told me about was the one involving her telephone. She said that for a while her phone would begin clicking at 4:24 a.m. every night as if someone was dialing it. Now it sounded like a rotary phone being dialed, but Mary did not have a rotary phone in her bedroom, she has a touch-tone push-button phone. Each time this would happen it would awaken Mary and she would check the time. It was always the same time. One night, Mary got brave and picked up the phone while it was clicking; there was no dial tone. Mary knew that no one was there to play tricks on her. Her husband was asleep beside her and her children are all grown and out on their own.

Mary racked her mind trying to find a reasonable explanation for these phenomena. Finally, she went to the local telephone company, described what she heard, and asked if they could explain it. The president of the company himself insisted that since Mary has a private line nothing like she described could happen. A lineman she asked also insisted that what she described was impossible. Mary got angry when she felt they did not believe her, so she set about proving that she did hear that odd noise.

She borrowed her adult son's cassette tape player and put it on the headboard of her bed. Whenever she heard the sounds, she would instantly reach up to push the record button. Mary is a smart lady and not only did she want to prove she heard the sounds, but she wanted to find out what numbers were being dialed. She set the machine on half speed so that she could slow down the clicking enough that she could count the clicks. Anyone who is familiar with the old rotary phones knows that if you count the clicks they correspond to the number being dialed. One click is for the number one, two clicks for the number two and so on, and Mary knew this. After taping the phantom phone call several times and noting the exact time, she began counting the clicks. Whoever was dialing those early morning calls was calling 227-9256. Now this telephone number only confused things further for to get an outside exchange from Mary's home requires dialing a 4-digit prefix. The only explanation that Mary could come up with was that when she had first moved into the area over 40 yrs. ago they had not had to dial any exchange. Perhaps whoever was dialing that number did not know that today that number could not be reached by dialing it that way.

Through time, other people have also heard the phone number being dialed. One of Mary's adult daughters spent a night at home and was awakened when the phone at her bedside also began the eerie clicking in the early morning hours. Mary's husband has heard it and once, her son also heard it. By this time, Mary had realized that if someone were in the basement dialing the only rotary phone left on the property, then every push-button phone would begin to click. Mary and her son both awoke one night while the phone was clicking and immediately they decided to catch this person. Together they quickly and quietly crept down the stairs to the basement, but no one was there. The whole house, basement included, was locked tight.

Recently the phone has not been clicking, but that does not change the fact that someone was dialing a number from the basement of Mary's home. Nor does that answer the question of who was dialing this number each night at 4:24 a.m. By the way, no such number has ever shown up on Mary's phone bill, so whoever was dialing never completed their connection. Given the history of Lillie and Glen Showalter, I could not help wondering if Lillie had tried to call for help before Glen murdered her. Is she still frantically trying to get help?

Though the phone has not clicked for some time, there has been a great deal of other phenomena that has continued. In recent years, one of Mary's daughter's has become interested in the paranormal and one evening when she was home this daughter and Mary went outside and began taking pictures. Mary has a digital camera, and this night the mother and daughter used both a 35mm and the digital cameras. The result of the photo session was amazing. Behind Mary's home sets a satellite dish and all around it they have repeatedly captured orbs. This would have been interesting if they captured an orb just once or twice, but Mary and her daughter, along with other people, myself included, have repeatedly captured multiple orbs. It is as if there is a group of spirits living in the area.

Now, the idea of a spirit community would be completely ridiculous if it would not be for the fact that this area is near where Mary has been told an Indian village once stood. Mary believes that these Indian spirits might be responsible for the odd red and yellow-orange streaks or orbs that she has captured on film.

Something at this place has also shown a great interest in the summerhouse. Mary and I have both captured orbs sitting atop this old house which no longer has electricity. She has a photograph where there is an orange glow in the shape of a window, again when there is no electricity in the house, and there has been a great deal of phenomena such as orbs between the bushes where the shed sat where Lillie's suicide had been faked

Mary agreed to allow me to investigate this phenomenon for myself. She told me that she had noticed the photographable phenomenon was more active around the time of the new moon. I made arrangements for Becky to come to Mary's house with me.

Becky often feels the presence of paranormal phenomena, and in the summerhouse she had terrible reactions and refused to go any further. She felt that something bad had happened there. She seemed to believe that perhaps this was one of the places where Lillie's daughter, Dora had been molested and she sensed a terrible fight between Dora and Glen Showalter.

About three weeks later, another sensitive member of the group, Al Brindza and his wife Jo accompanied me to Mary's home for a second night of investigating. This time it was when the moon was nearly full. It was a calm, clear summer night with high visibility,

Orb on the roof of the original home of Lillie Wright Showalter

and there was very little phenomena outside. A few impressions of being watched, but on the whole those can easily be dismissed as nerves and imagination, after all, we were in a place where terrible crimes had occurred.

Al, who has a physical reaction of feeling dizzy in the presence of strong paranormal phenomena, felt very odd inside the summerhouse and he had to leave because whatever force was in there was hostile. (I am finding that people sensitive to this phenomenon often react by feeling dazed or dizzy, as if something is disrupting their equilibrium. That feeling of dizziness forced him to leave the building. His wife and I felt nothing in particular.

Al decided to return to the house a second time, but he still felt this dizziness in the vicinity of the stairs. The summerhouse is a very small building consisting of a small room, a set of stairs and a single small room upstairs. It was the first structure known to be on the property, and was where Lillie and her first husband, Orville, had lived while building the present house.

Al insisted that he stay in the building for a bit longer. He was taking temperature readings at the top of the stairs and we were in the dark except for the occasional use of a small flashlight that his wife held. I began to talk to whatever entity might be there and called out several names. I spoke to Showalter, Dora, and Lillie and for some reason I kept hearing the name Anderson and called that one out softly. When I did that, the flash-

Al under the influence of the spirit at Lillie Wright Showalter's first home

light suddenly flickered and dimmed almost off. I kept speaking to this "something" and the light went dead.

Suddenly Al, at the foot of the stairs, called out and I thought that perhaps he was encountering something so I clicked three quick photos. The interior of the building was pitch black without the flashlight, but the flash of the camera revealed that Al was pushed against the wall, half-standing half slumping as he struggled. Suddenly he shouted, "Help me; get me out of here!" His voice was panicked and Jo and I immediately grabbed him and dragged him from the building. In seconds, he was sitting on the porch and struggling to tell us what had happened.

When I had seen his face in the flash, I had feared he was having a heart attack. It

85

was a terrible moment because I had never even considered such a thing before. Now, thankfully, he told us that it was the entity in there that had disoriented him.

While he recovered on the porch, his wife and I returned to the building. Neither of us felt anything tangible, but there was an edge in the air. (Again, that could have been nerves or imagination.) We did not see or feel anything at that time. In minutes, Al returned. (If nothing else, Al is dedicated and determined and I'm grateful for that.) Suddenly, he made a cry and we heard a thud at the same time something unseen brushed past me toward the door where there was full moonlight streaming in. There was nothing to be seen, but I clearly felt something brush past me. Jo also felt the same thing. What went out that door? I do not think I'll ever know.

This story was further complicated when, a couple weeks later, psychic Kelly Weaver, who is now a friend, came up with her husband John. They had told me that they wanted to visit a few haunted sites. The last spot I took them to was Mary's home.

Kelly walked into the summerhouse and up the stairs. Neither she nor John felt anything "evil." In fact, Kelly came away saying that she had talked to the one spirit on the second floor of the old summerhouse. A spirit she described as an older fellow with a balding pate and a fringe of white hair was sitting in an old rocking chair smoking a corn-cob pipe and cracking peanuts. The shells were all around him on the floor. The old fellow was wearing a well-worn flannel shirt and she said he told her that he had really enjoyed sitting there like that during the last part of his life. She saw another fellow in bed. He wore blue pajamas and was dying of some respiratory disease. She said she could hear him wheezing. What Kelly did not find was that entity that so frightened my friends. Kelly came away feeling only love in the building. When Kelly spoke to Mary about these impressions, Mary immediately knew whom these two men were. Orville Wright had died of pneumonia in the building so it was reasonable to suspect that he was the man with the respiratory disease. The other man made Mary smile. He was the old man whom she had bought the house from. She could well remember him in his flannel shirts sitting in the little house. She remembered how his wife had complained that she could barely get him out of those old shirts. She remembered, too, his ruff of white hair on his otherwise bald head, and his penchant for going to the summerhouse for a smoke.

Kelly also picked up on Indian ceremonies, "a lot of them," in the area where the satellite dish now sits. Here is where Mary believes the Indian cemetery was. Kelly described scaffolds with bodies upon them. This was accurate as most of the Indians of Pennsylvania did lay their dead up on scaffolds.

Kelly described someone who she believed was white hiding in the bushes in the area where people have captured red energy on film. She saw a white shirt or nightgown and several people hiding.

Before the summerhouse, she passed a particular bush and instantly had a headache. "Someone was hit on the head hard here," she said before quickly stepping away from that area and the pain.

She also described seeing smoke from a distant Indian village, a village upon the hill where past owners have dug up so many relics and she distinctly heard Indian drums.

Behind the summerhouse where the tool shed had been, where Lillie had been found dead, Kelly felt something falling down into a pit or down onto the ground. Here, she heard a word that sounded like "Trader" said very loudly. She could not make out why this word had been said so loudly just in front of her.

When Kelly was done with her tour of the area, we rejoined Mary on her porch. Until now, I had been vague and rather uncommucative. I believed that Mary deserved to tell

Kelly the story of her home herself. While she told Kelly about the Indian relics found on the property, where she had photographed orbs, and the story of Lillie, Kelly kept nodding. She and John asked some questions to verify impressions.

Kelly described an animal pen or shack behind the old garden tool shack where Lillie had died. She said she heard goats or sheep (she could not tell which) in that area. She also said that she saw a white picket fence around the property. Mary shook her head on this one. She had never known of such a fence. However, a few days after Kelly's visit Mary had an opportunity to talk to a niece of Lillie's named Ruth who verified that such a picket fence with a gate had existed around the property in Lillie's time. Ruth was only four years old when Lillie had been murdered, but she had lived above Lillie's home and remembered hearing the shot because he father had commented upon it. She also saw the body because her family had taken a walk down to Lillie's right after the shot and came upon the body just after Erwin had found his mother.

Mary invited us inside for a cup of coffee in her kitchen and asked John and Kelly if they'd like to see the photos she had taken at her home. While we were in the kitchen, Kelly confided to me that she was being touched by a woman who was patting her hair and who was touching her shoulders. She also heard voices talking, but she could not make out the words. This I found quite interesting because on a recent visit to Mary's home, my teenaged son had experienced the same phenomena. Twice he had asked me if I heard voices talking when Mary left the room. I did not. I asked what they were saying, but he said it wasn't English. After a while, my son leaned over and said, "Mom, it almost sounds like Grandma's Dances With Wolves tape when the Indians talk, but not quite." Could they be hearing the voices of the long dead natives who had been in the cemetery where the house and yard now are?

When I spoke to Lillie's niece, Ruth, she confided to me that, on the eve of the anniversary of her aunt's death in the year 2000, she had been to visit Mary. She had been to the house countless times through the years. She had been a friend of the previous owners, too, and she had been there in Lillie's time. Upon this visit, something remarkable happened to Ruth--something that she had not yet confided to anyone.

When she left Mary's house, she walked down the flag stones at the side of the house near the summerhouse. Suddenly, a terrible fear overwhelmed her. It was a feeling that she had ever experienced. Ruth felt a strong urge to turn and run back into Mary's house. She felt complete panic, as if she had to hurry and hide. She told me that she remembered thinking about going back into the house, but that the car was closer, so she ran to that. Once inside, Ruth felt compelled to lock the doors and hurry away. This whole time she was terribly cold. Ruth has never been one to complain of the cold and never in her life had she felt such a chill. Ruth slammed the door locks (something she never did) and hurried out the road. Furthermore, this happened on a warm evening. These terrible feelings lasted until she was home, and even for a short while after that. It was such a remarkable feeling of evil and fear that she found it profoundly difficult to tell people about it. She believes that she had experienced this feeling because it was the eve of the anniversary of Lillie's death. This evil she felt had been something her aunt had felt the night she had died.

For her part, Mary is not frightened in the house or on the grounds. She often takes her camera with her and walks the property at night just to see what develops. She is more curious than scared and she has made living with Lillie just another part of her already full life.

WHAT WALKS AT
CAPTAIN PHILLIPS?

(Huntingdon County)

Most folks have heard of historic sites that are supposed to be haunted because of some historic event. Fort Miflin and the Jean Bonnet Tavern are two such sites, and so is Captain Phillip's Monument. I have long heard the stories, but when the Central Pennsylvania Paranormal Association and I went to this site in August of 2000, I held little hope of finding a spirit. After all, I had been there countless times through the years. It was an eerie spot admittedly, but I always attributed that to the lonesome location, and to the fact that I knew of the many horrific events that had occurred there. Despite the fact that I love a good ghost story, I am not gullible and I don't see ghost coming out of the walls everywhere I go. I really did not believe Captain Phillip's Monument was haunted, but that was before this visit.

Captain William Phillips was a veteran of the American Revolution who had settled upon Clover Creek road in present day Blair County between Williamsburg and Fredericksburg. In 1780, Indian raids in the area of Bedford County (out which Blair and Huntingdon along with Fulton County were culled) were so numerous as to make even tax collecting impossible. Travel had virtually come to a standstill, and matters were growing desperate for the farmers who had to harvest their crops in those remote valleys under attack.

For their part, the Indians were infuriated and responding to both attacks upon their settlements and violations of the land rights that they had negotiated. These agreements restricted the areas where Europeans could live so that the natives could keep control of areas where their villages and best hunting lands were. The way the Indians were being treated by the Europeans was both unfair and deadly. This made the natives extremely angry, and in their culture, vengeance was an honored way of dealing with such unscrupulous enemies.

Colonel John Piper of Piper's Fort on Yellow Creek (on Route 26 below Everett, Bedford County) recognized the situation and wrote to the President of Pennsylvania explaining the situation, and asking for arms and militia to put down the natives. While President Wharton was considering this request, John Piper wrote a letter to Captain William Phillips telling him to muster a force of Rangers and go to Woodcock Valley (near Saxton) to protect the farmers there who had to harvest their crops.

John Piper had many reasons for choosing Captain Phillips for this job. Phillips was a man who was well liked and respected by the other colonial families, and he had a good reputation among the natives for being a fair man. This reputation, Colonel Piper hoped, would protect Phillips and his Rangers from attack.

Captain Phillips left for Woodcock Valley on Saturday, July 15, with ten rangers and his fourteen-year-old son. Despite his best efforts, Captain Phillips could not convince more of the settlers to accompany him. These people had their own families to consider and could not be bothered with risking their lives for others. This might seem selfish in today's age, but these settlers had to fear that if they left their families and farms unprotected they would be attacked by Indians who also were in the Clover Creek area. There had already been several massacres there.

For his part, Captain Phillips must have realized that ten Rangers were not enough to do much with, but he was a man of honor and had given his word to Colonel John Piper that he would do his best to protect the farmers of Woodcock Valley. He would do so even if it meant his own death.

Phillips and his men marched over Tussey's Mountain into the valley only to find the first few isolated cabins were already abandoned. He and his men went further into the valley, but it soon was obvious that the settlers had all abandoned their homes for safety elsewhere. By the time that they had reconnoitered the valley it was growing late. The men were all on foot and must have been tired. Captain Phillips knew a man in the valley named Frederick Keeter well. He decided that they would spend the night in the Keeter cabin. So far, they had met no one. Even the Indians were seemingly not in evidence at this point. Captain Phillips must have truly believed that it was safe to remain in Woodcock Valley or he would not have risked so many lives, including his own son's life.

The men put in an uneventful night camped upon the floor of the little cabin. In the morning, though, matters were taken from Captain Phillip's hands. He and his men awoke to find that during the night the cabin had been surrounded by Indians who were seemingly unaware of their presence. They looked out of little gun slots in the walls, which had been constructed instead of windows, and saw two white men who had "gone native" in the group. Captain Phillips realized instantly that he and his men were out manned and out gunned. Their only hope was to pray that the Indians did not realize that the cabin was inhabited and that they would pass on. He instructed his men to keep a sharp watch and maintain silence at all costs.

The day wore on in silence. The tension within that little cabin must have been unbearable for as the day progressed the Indians were making forays ever nearer. The men knew that most probably they would be discovered, and that must have made the waiting more terrible. At last, in the afternoon, two Indians and the two whites with them came very close to the cabin. One of the Rangers seemed to loose his nerve and began shooting. He hit one of the Indians with his bullet. Now, the men inside the cabin were committed to a battle. Within seconds the Indians had taken positions around the cabin and began firing. A spate of gunfire erupted and lasted for about ten minutes. Then there was a terrible silence as the two sides regrouped.

Phillips knew that his men were not prepared to face a siege, and that soon the Indians would come again. He hoped to hold them off long enough to make some sort of arrangement with them. There was shooting back and forth for a while, but the Indians did not seem to want to waste precious ammunition upon the whites. They had a better idea. Suddenly, the men inside the cabin saw flaming arrows come in their direction. The arrows set the little wooden cabin on fire. Captain Phillip's time was up. He now had to surrender or burn to death.

Captain Phillips called out that he wanted to bargain. The whites with the Indians interpreted for Phillips and he offered to surrender. However, he had terms that the Indians had to agree to. They would surrender and give up their weapons if they would be promised that no physical harm would come to them.

The Indians agreed to this bargain and Phillips and his men stepped from the burning cabin. His men were tied up and herded together. The men began walking in the direction their captors indicated. They seemed to be going back toward Tussey's Mountain. Near the foot of the mountain, however, Phillips and his son were separated and started up the side of the mountain. Despite his protests, his men were left behind with the bulk of the Indians. Later, Captain Phillips would write about how helpless he felt as he and his son trudged on. Behind him he could hear shooting and screaming and he could well imagine what fate was befalling his men. He could do nothing to help them. The Indians had kept him and his son safe, but someone had to pay for shooting and wounding some of their men. He would never know if any of the wounded died, but something had transpired which had caused the Indians to separate the men and brutally mutilate them. Phillips and his son would survive. They were taken to an Indian town near modern day Frankstown in Blair County and then up into New York where they would stay for two years until they were ransomed back to the whites.

Days later, Colonel Piper would bring a force of men with him as he rode into Woodcock Valley in search of Captain Phillips. What they found near the foot of the mountain was savage enough to sicken the toughest, war hardened veteran among them. Phillip's Rangers had all been tied to trees. Then they had been cut open slowly and mutilated while alive. The bodies had been left tied where they had suffered so. Now, the corpses were blackened and bloated. The men ordered to cut them down would be able to tell who died first and who died last. It seemed that the last man had witnessed so much that he had gone insane with fear. He had literally tried so hard to pull free of his bonds that the rawhide binding him had cut into his very bones. It was truly a terrible and pitiful sight.

Today, a monument sits as tribute to the deaths of these men. It is upon the very site of the massacre and this was confirmed when during the building process for the monument the workers came upon nine of the ten bodies of the murdered Rangers. The identity of the bodies was confirmed by the age of the bones, and by dating of the buckles and buttons that were on the corpses. The tenth body was not found for some reason. The nine corpses now rest in a common grave upon the very monument itself. It is there as mute testimony to another time when one culture was struggling desperately to keep it's hold on it's world, and another society was determined to take the very land the natives needed for existence.

Capt. Phillip's Monument area where native spirit stood
by Carolyn Hedges

Through the years, a legend has endured that Captain Phillip's Rangers haunt the site. It has long been claimed that upon the anniversary of the massacre late at night the brutal murders are relived and the men who died and the Indians who killed them are seen and heard once more. I have been there several times on that night, but have seen and heard nothing. Of course, I'm about as psychically inclined as a box of rocks most of the time. However, that seems to be changing, but that is another story...

When some friends and I started the Central Pennsylvania Paranormal Association, one of the first sites we chose was Captain Phillip's Monument. My reasoning for doing so, was that I really did not believe it was haunted and I wanted the group members to understand early on that we will have sites like that. However, I was to be the one surprised.

The group met there in August of 2000. The members were Jim and Carolyn, Al and Joanne Brindza, Jeanette and myself. It was a pleasant evening and the site is remote enough that you feel alone there. A cool evening breeze had sprung up, and as we walked

Al at Capt. Phillip's photo by Carolyn Hedges

around the site I began to feel watched. It was a distinct feeling that someone was on the far-left side of the monument, just beyond the tree line curiously watching our every move. Since I was in a group, I went over and looked the area over well. There were certainly no trees large enough for a man to hide behind, but here the feeling of being watched was even stronger. Suddenly I was struck by the strong impression of a Native man with rawhide pants and shirt, a hair knot with feathers and shaved sides of his head. He had a strong hawk face with slashes of paint on his cheeks and under his eyes, but the strongest feeling I had was that he was lonely and afraid of us.

I decided not to mention the feeling of being watched unless someone else did first. Apparently Al was feeling the same thing that I was for eventually, he came to me and asked if I was sure that Phillip's Rangers were supposed to haunt this site. I shrugged and just muttered, "That's what they say."

Al eyed me warily and sighed. "I know that this will sound crazy, but I keep sensing an Indian man back there watching us." He pointed toward the left rear corner of the monument. It was the same area where I had sensed the fellow.

I could not help myself, "What does he look like?" I asked softly.

Al looked off in that direction for a few seconds. "He has deer hide pants and he's tall and slim. He has a hawk nose and a lump or knot in his hair with feathers sticking out of it. The sides are shaved and I think there's paint on his face. It's hard to tell because he's in the shadows." He had just described the fellow I had seen!

We pulled up our cameras and kept snapping photos of that area. (Later, one team member would find that of the three rolls of film he had taken only a few photos came out. The rest were blank. Another team member had a strange haze appear on all of her photos that obscured the image. This seemed extremely odd as it was a clear summer night and there was not one tendril of fog in that area.)

As the evening wore on, Carolyn suddenly had a sensation of cold chills as if something had just passed by her, and she started clicking away. We saw something shadowy moving toward her, but it disappeared immediately.

When we had first arrived, we had set up one cassette recorder on the left rear portion of the monument, one on the left foreground of the monument, and a third voice activated machine on the right side just past the monument. For some time the machines worked well, but as it grew darker the machines suddenly began to give us trouble. Our three cassette tape players kept turning themselves off. The new batteries in each died after only an hour and a half.

Our equipment troubles were just beginning. We had a camera that, though just loaded with film, spontaneously rewound itself. My digital camera took several good photos, and then one that had supercharged energy in the trees where we felt watched. After that, the rest of the photos became just a jumble of color.

At one point, we heard a strange animal yell that none of us could identify. Now most of us have lived in the country all of our lives and at least one member of the group was a hunter, yet no one could recognize that distinctive yelp. Later Carolyn would confide to me that she thought instantly of all those old movies where an animal call was made by Indians just before they attacked. She laughed and said how silly that idea was. Neither Al nor I had mentioned this to anyone else that night in the group for fear of tainting the observations of the rest of the group.

Near ten o'clock the group moved slightly away from the site to the area where Carolyn had felt the cold spot. At that time, we began chatting as we looked back at the monument to see if the cassette players were working now that we had changed batteries in each of them. In the darkness we could not see the machines, but we could see the red dot from the record light on two of the machines. As we watched, we suddenly saw the one machine's light blink out as if something had come between the machine and our eyes. Immediately after that, the machine appeared to rotate about thirty degrees as if someone had bumped or pushed it slightly. We hurried back and examined the machine. It was certainly moved from the position we had left it in. The new batteries were also drained although they had only been in the machine for less than thirty minutes.

After that, it was as if whoever had been so curious about the recorders had retreated. Though we again moved away from the monument and waited, we did not see any further activity. We finally left before the mosquitoes could finish their dinner of ghost hunter delight.

Becky Gummo had not been able to go with us for this visit, but a week later, Becky, her husband and I returned to the sight for a second look. Becky had always been fascinated by the area, and she immediately felt something in the same spot where Al and I had on a previous visit.

Becky snapped several photos and so did I. Once again, I was overwhelmed by that feeling of being watched by a man, but I tried not to say anything. After walking the site for a while, Becky and I sat on the steps of the monument and began to talk. I expressed sympathy for this man whom I believed must be waiting for something. Perhaps for his fellow Indians to return from wherever they had gone so long ago. Suddenly Becky seemed to be looking behind me. "Patty," she whispered, "turn around slowly and take a look."

I turned and saw a black shadow that seemed to be hunkered down on one knee watching. As I turned, it stood up and stepped back into the darkness of the trees. "Did you see that black shadow?" I asked.

"He was watching, listening to us," Becky replied softly.

We resumed our conversation and once more I expressed sympathy for this fellow. I am part Native American and I have always been conflicted about the struggle that caused America to be born. I do understand why the Indians did what they did at that spot, even if it seems brutal. As I spoke, I suddenly felt something cold literally clutch my right hand. I stopped, startled and looked at Becky.

"Something's got my hand," I said softly. She reached over and felt my hand. There was a pocket of cold air wrapped around it. As we sat there, another pocket of cold air slipped around my left hand and again, Becky could feel it. My fingers were like ice and it was late August. It had to be at least 72 degrees out that evening. I felt that this man was holding my hands; it was as if he was drawn by my sympathy for him and his situation.

After a few seconds, the cold let go of my left hand, then my right. Whatever had touched me had moved back once more.

Now, Becky was feeling a bit unnerved and the mosquitoes were once again dining on us, so we returned to the van where her husband was waiting. As we sat there, I kept watching out the van window and several times I saw a dim shadow break away from the trees and pace near the van. Once, it completely circled the van and Becky felt it, too. She kept insisting that I pray for protection before I leave this place and that I tell this entity that it must stay there. She was feeling very protective of me at that moment. We both saw the shadow as if he was waiting for me to come out of the metal box I was in.

When I went back to my van, Becky's husband made sure it was safe. I did pray and I spoke softly to this entity and asked it to stay. I know it must be lonely there, but I knew that I did not want to deal with it coming home with me.

I have not been back since that night, only because I have been so very busy, but I do plan to go back there at some point. I was unnerved by what I had experienced, but not truly frightened. I still feel very sorry for whoever is there. I pray that he will find his way onward and find peace at last. He seemed more sad than frightening to me.

If someone asked me if Capt. Phillip's monument is haunted, I'd have to say that personally I believe it is. But I would also add that not all ghosts are fearful and this one could do with some sympathy rather than the fear that has so often greeted it in the past.

GRAY EYES

(Allegheny County)

In the early spring of 2000, I received a letter from a woman who sounded quite frightened. She wrote that she had two ghosts in her home and was afraid of the one she called Gray Eyes. She went on to say that she had not even realized that the house was haunted when she had first moved into it. It was a home that belonged to her new husband and his former wife. She had heard a few rumors that it might have been haunted, but certainly there was not any warning that had prepared her for what she was about to encounter.

The woman, *Carolyn, had been fascinated by the idea that her home might be haunted, but for the first year she lived there she felt and saw nothing to indicate that the rumors were true. Apparently this home had fallen victim to the rumor mill that labels certain homes "haunted" for no good reason.

However, this was all about to change. Carolyn began to notice that small things were being moved about in her home. At first, the items were barely noticeable, but when she asked her husband, *David, about it, he would always deny that he had moved the items. Soon after this happened, Carolyn began to notice that she was feeling a cold spot which moved around the house. Though this was disconcerting, she did not really believe that there was anything to fear. In fact, she felt that whoever was nearby was an elderly woman who meant her and her husband no harm. Within months she began seeing a shadow moving by out of the corner of her eye when she was alone. Though her husband had originally been the one to tell of the rumors that his home was haunted, he did not want to hear about her tales of shadow figures, cold spots and items moved just a little bit as if another woman was adding her own touch to the house.

Carolyn began to research the property and found that the house had belonged to an elderly maiden lady named *Sarah who had died there. This woman had lived her whole life in the house. Sarah had inherited the house upon her parent's death. She had never married, and had always cared for her aged parents. When Sarah had died, her extended family no longer wanted to keep the old homestead and it had been put up for sale. Carolyn's husband and his first wife had bought the house and lived there until the divorce. Now, Carolyn believed that her ghost was that of this elderly woman, Sarah, and she felt that this haunting was benign.

Since David did not want to hear about the ghost, Carolyn turned to her friends. No matter how nice the ghost, it was still a disconcerting thing to find yourself sharing your home with the spirit of another and she needed someone to talk to about it. One of her friends fancied himself an amateur psychic and was very much into the use of ouija boards and seances. This fellow, *Al, suggested that they try to contact Sarah and find out why she was haunting the house.

Carolyn had played with the ouija board a few times and she thought that this was a fun idea. In fact, as it was now the fall of 1999 she proposed that they use the ouija board and hold a seance as part of a Halloween party.

The night for the party rolled around and Carolyn was prepared. She had invited several friends; Al included, to this night's festivities. They had dinner, then cleared the table. Several people tried to work the ouija board with Al but they had little success. Finally,

Carolyn placed her fingers upon the planchette and it literally took off. Within moments they were talking to Sarah. She began to tell them that she was there as a protective spirit and that another haunted the house as well. Al asked who this spirit was and why did Sarah needed to protect them from it. Suddenly the planchette stopped dead. Sarah, or something, had cut off communication!

Later that night, Carolyn and her guests joined hands around her dining room table as Al asked the spirits to come to him. It was a scene right out of a movie; candles flickered upon the table and around the perimeter the darkness was broken only by that fragile light. Suddenly a deep voice took over Al's softer sounds. This entity said that it's name was *Samuel Hanks and that he was a soldier during World War Two. He sounded angry and confused and kept demanding to know why these people were in *Alice's home. Alice, he said, was his fiancee. He told them that he wanted to speak to Alice immediately. As no one knew whom he meant, they could not help him. Samuel went away angry.

Carolyn would not have long to wonder what she had stirred up with Samuel. That very night she awoke startled. She felt as if someone's eyes were boring into her. She rolled over and froze. Standing on her side of the bed, glaring down at her, was a man in a World War Two bomber's jacket and Air Force uniform. She saw the uniform, though she did not exactly recognize it yet, and kept looking up until she came to the man's face. His most prominent feature was his eyes. They were a deep, slate gray and they flashed pure hatred at her. Carolyn reached out to wake David, but he was sleeping soundly. Carolyn felt pinned by those gray eyes and unable to move; at last she let out a cry and David sat up rubbing his face.

In a rush Carolyn poured out her story, but David did not want to hear it. He had been against this seance idea and now he blamed Carolyn for bad dreams brought on by messing with stuff she should have let alone. Carolyn finally drifted back into an uneasy sleep, but she could not help wondering if David was right? Had she imagined that man with the intense hatred in his gray eyes?

When nothing happened for a couple days, Carolyn began to relax. David must have been right. She had conjured up Gray Eyes after that seance and ouija board session. However, only a couple days later she was walking down the second floor hall when the door to the attic opened. A young man wearing a bomber jacket, a military uniform and boots stepped through the door. He turned toward her and she gasped. He had steely gray eyes. The man turned and walked down the hall toward the bathroom. He disappeared through that door.

Carolyn fought feeling paralyzed and flew to the door. There was no way out of the bathroom except the hall door. She jerked it open, but the room was empty.

After that day she would repeatedly see the man coming from the semi-finished attic and going down into the body of the house. Though he often glared at her, he never said a word--for which she was very glad. So far, she had been alone in her experiences and she knew that David was more than skeptical about the idea of a gray-eyed ghost. In fact, David was downright hostile to the idea.

For Carolyn the nights were the worst. She often awoke feeling watched and rolled over to see Gray Eyes watching her. Each time he simply faded away, leaving her with a feeling of the intense hatred that exuded from him. She was very frightened of Gray Eyes.

Carolyn no longer felt the warming presence of Sarah either. No longer were things slightly out of place, and she did not see the shadowy form of the older woman. She could not help wondering if Gray Eyes had somehow subdued her.

One day Al came to visit and Carolyn debated about telling him of the new entity in the house, but she chose not to speak. She did not want people to think she was crazy. Al went upstairs to the bathroom, but when he came back he looked ashen, shaken. He told Carolyn that when he was in the hallway, the door to the attic had suddenly opened and a man in a bomber jacket and uniform came out. The man had gone down the hall a little way, turned to look back at Al with a look of dislike, then disappeared. "Who was that?" Al demanded.

Now, Carolyn was truly glad that she had not confided in Al. His testimony might help convince David. But David would not believe Al either. After all, hadn't he participated in the antics that had started the nightmares?

Through the following weeks, David and Carolyn would have a series of guests who would return to them shaken and frightened. Each person told the same story of hearing footsteps on the attic stairs, of the attic doorknob turning, of a man in a bomber's jacket and military uniform coming through the door. They described the man as young, and they all said that he had deep gray eyes that had looked at them angrily. By now, even David had to admit that something was going on. He was tired from Carolyn's nearly nightly visits from the spirit, but one night he would discover exactly why she felt such fear.

On that night, Carolyn was sleeping a sleep of total exhaustion when David heard her muttering in her sleep. He roused to wake her and tell her that she was having bad dreams. As he rolled toward Carolyn he froze. There, beside the bed watching them sleep was the man Carolyn had been seeing. Now David had become a believer.

The young couple set rules in place that there would be no more seances or ouija board sessions in their home. They tried not to talk about ghosts or haunting in hopes that if he was ignored he might go away. It did not seem to help.

One day Carolyn was in town when she met a woman who was a niece of Sarah's. The woman asked her questions about the old family homestead. She said that her mother, who had grown up there, had expressed a wish to visit the place once more. Carolyn invited them to come anytime. Soon this woman took her up on the offer and brought her mother over for a visit.

The older lady walked through the house and told many family stories. She described happy scenes of growing up there. She was one of three daughters who had been raised in that house. She told Carolyn that aside from herself there was her sister, Sarah and her older sister Alice. Now Carolyn knew who Alice was.

While they sat in the living room, Carolyn carefully brought the topic back to Alice and the past. By now, she had looked up the uniform that the phantom wore and knew that it was that of the Air Force during WWII. She asked if Alice had been married in the house.

The older woman shook her head sadly. "No," she said, "Alice had not married while we lived here. In fact, there is a very sad story associated with Alice and that topic. You see Alice was engaged to be married to a fellow named *Samuel Hanks, but when WWII broke out, he joined up. He had been a pilot in civilian life and soon had become one for the military as well. On furloughs, he would come to visit Alice. Mother and Father had a small room fixed up in the attic for him and he'd stay there. However, not long before they were to have married, Sam was suddenly shipped out. He died when his plane crashed on some Japanese island. Alice never knew much about his death, but it was very hard for her. She cried a lot and kept saying that Sam would never leave her. It took a long time for Alice to find love again."

While the older woman spoke, Carolyn became aware of a shadow gliding down the stairs. It was the figure of the old woman Carolyn had always believed was Sarah. Had Sarah come to visit with her sister? Carolyn did not say a word as the old woman came up behind her little sister. For a few brief seconds, the spirit laid her hand upon her little sister's shoulder, then disappeared. Carolyn never mentioned it to the couple, as she did not want to upset the older lady.

Now Carolyn believed she knew the identity of the ghost man, but that did not protect her from his evil, glaring stare that disturbed her sleep. He had managed to slide into her very dreams at night. Several times, she had awakened from nightmares of the man only to find him glaring at her before he faded away.

One night Carolyn dreamt that the spirit was lying on top of David. For some reason, this upset her greatly. She shook herself awake fearing that he might smother her husband. She shook David just to be sure that he was okay. It took a terribly long time to awake her husband, and when he turned over she let out a scream. Though David had lovely blue eyes, they had suddenly become gray and the expression on his face was the same sullen one she had seen so often upon the spirit's countenance. She screamed and jumped from bed. Within seconds, her cries had seemed to drive the spirit out and David's eyes returned to their bright blue. After that night, the couple began sleeping in shifts. This way one person would remain awake to watch over the sleeping person.

All of this had led Carolyn to write to me asking for help. She said that they were frightened and tired and she was heartily sorry that she had ever disturbed this entity. I called Carolyn immediately and offered her what help I could. We spoke once and she told me everything I have imparted. I called to follow up and see if the person I had told her to contact had helped her. Carolyn never returned my call. I wrote to her again offering her the help she needed. I have never heard from Carolyn again. Has something happened to her? Did the ghost drive her away? Unlike with fiction where every loose end must be neatly tired up, in real life sometimes there are no good answers. I am only relating the story as I took it from my notes and her letter. I hope that Carolyn and David are fine and did not answer my letter because they did not want any more to do with the entity. I simply offer them my prayers that they are okay.

LIZZIE'S HOUSE

(Exeter, Luzerne County)

Ghost stories often drift from the realm of the factual to the fictional. Names are lost and information becomes blurred with time. Many old ghost stories are that way. So it is with Lizzie's story. Though the nexus of it is true, the story is also part of Pennsylvania's rich tapestry of folklore. You will have to decide how much you will believe for yourself, but there is little doubt that Lizzie does haunt her former home.

So many ghost stories are born of tragedy and the weaknesses of human nature. Lizzie's story is no exception. She thought that she and her husband were very lucky people. They were happy, prosperous and in love. Her husband provided for her enough so that she could afford the luxury of a housekeeper to do the day to day drudgework. Lizzie thought she had her home in order.

However, her whole world came apart one day when she found out that the efficient housekeeper who lived in her home had taken Lizzie's own husband as her lover. Lizzie did not know who was at fault, who had pursued whom, but she was devastated. She sought out her husband in the upstairs hallway near their bedroom and threw her knowledge at him. To her surprise her husband did not deny the affair. He confessed the entire thing; then he told Lizzie that this was not some casual fling for them. He had fallen in love with the housekeeper and wanted to go off with her. He wanted a divorce!

There was a terrible fight. Lizzie was infuriated and she screamed that she'd never divorce him; she'd never be shamed in this way. The fight became physical as they struggled not only with the betrayal and the emotional turmoil that it had caused, but now they struggled for physical control.

In a powerful thrust Lizzie's husband pushed her away and she fell down the stairs. If he meant to kill her we will never know, but that was what he did do. Her body, broken and bleeding, lay at the bottom of the stairs like a rag doll someone had tossed away.

The scandal of a dead wife and a mistress in the same home took its toll. Lizzie's husband lost everything and was tried for murder. The house gained a reputation and it became vacant. Through the years, ghost stories grew up around the place. Of course, such stories were bound to surface about a death house like this one on Lincoln Road.

The stories would have eventually died away except that those who trespassed into Lizzie's home and tried to live there found themselves confronted by a ghostly Lizzie. Footsteps are heard in the house, a terrible thumping as if someone is falling down the stairs has often been reported, and lights flicker off and on. Others have told of hearing loud screeches or screams late in the night. It seems that Lizzie has never left her home, and perhaps she is still reliving her death scene.

This would have been enough to ensure the haunted history of any house, but there is one more story of Lizzie's house that has made it even more infamous. Years after the murder had occurred a teenage boy was stopped in front of Lizzie's House on Lincoln Road by a car full of teenage boys. The carload of young men had been taunting the young man who was on foot. They quickly surrounded the lone teenager and beat him mercilessly. They demanded the boy's money, and they had every intention of beating and killing the boy. However, something caught the attention of one of the assailants. He looked up at the long vacant house and saw a woman watching them. Suddenly, the woman came through the wall very quickly and seemed to float in the direction of the attack. Screaming, the one thug took off. The other assailants caught sight of the strange floating figure in white and ran to their car, too.

A phone call was received only seconds later at the local police station. The woman said that a young boy had been savagely beaten in front of a house on Lincoln Road and told them to send help. The officer who took the call recorded that the woman would only give her first name--Lizzie.

Unfortunately, Lizzie had come too late to help the teenager who died in her front yard. However, Lizzie surely did her best to help him and it seemed to change the character of the haunting forever. Lizzie was no longer just a victim of a love triangle gone wrong; now she was a kind soul who had tried to save a young man in circumstances similar to her own.

The house is still not lived in, but at Halloween a local group runs a tour of Lizzie's house as a haunted house for the town. Most of the haunting at that time is very earthly in nature. There is the usual silliness of masked faces and dripping blood, but even then there are those who have reported seeing a white mass of fog within the house or outside when all else is clear. They report odd noises and stray sounds that no one can account for. Perhaps this Halloween haunted house is more authentic than it first seems.

THE WITCH'S CAVE

(Latrobe, Westmoreland County)

Those who grew up in the Latrobe area might remember a place known locally as the Witch's Cave. It was actually an old railroad tunnel that had been abandoned and obtained its name because of the way it looked. The area was often mist-shrouded and looked like "the gates of hell," or so I have been told by a local resident. This area became a hangout for the local teens in the area until it was finally filled in. A housing project went up nearby and the residents of the complex felt that the old tunnel was a dangerous place for their children. However, before the complex was built, there were many that knew the ghost story of the Witch's Cave.

Early in the twentieth century the tunnel was well used, but as railroading died out in favor of trucking goods to market, the tunnel became a place abandoned much of the time. There were only a couple trains a week that would go through that old tunnel. By the 1960's the trains had dwindled down to only one train every couple weeks.

A local man chose this spot because of its solitude to end his life, but if the stories are true, he never left there. The man took a rope to the Witch's Cave and tied one end of it to a tree that was growing atop the old tunnel. He fed the rope through a vent in the top of the tunnel and went down to pull it through. Then he stacked up some rocks and tied the other end around his neck. One short jump and he was dead.

No one thought to look in the old railroad tunnel when the man was reported missing. It was a few weeks before a train came hurling itself through the tunnel. The engineer was not even aware that he had struck the body dangling from the top of the tunnel. However, when he arrived at his destination they found half the mutilated corpse stuck to the train. By tracing back the train's route they found the top half of the body dangling from the strong rope.

Of course, such a grisly story was bound to cause tales to start up, and it didn't take long. People began talking about hearing thumps, banging, crying and shouting in the tunnel although there was no one inside it. Several braver folks investigated, but never found anything. Some folks attributed the ghastly sounds to the suicide that had taken place, but older folks could have told them that long before that man had ended his life others had heard similar sounds. Shrill screams, sobbing, heavy thuds and the like had helped give the tunnel its macabre name. Perhaps the suicide victim did haunt the site but if he did, then he only added another voice to those already suffering there.

No one knows exactly why the sounds came from the tunnel, and no local lore talks of the traditional things you would expect. No tales of train wrecks, Indian massacres or burial grounds are connected to this site. However, the stories of the strange sounds coming from the Witch's Cave persisted until the tunnel was filled up.

Did the spirits leave when the tunnel was filled in or do they now walk looking for a new home? No one knows for sure, but I would not be surprised if those who live in the new houses closest to the old train tunnel had a few stories of their own to tell.

THE TANGLED KNOTS
GHOSTS WEAVE

(Altoona, Blair County)

Sometimes from tragedy great joy can be born and old friends can begin a new relationship as lovers. Some people do get second chances at happiness, and that was how it was for *Katrina Smith. After her husband had died, she felt terribly alone and cut off, but a good family friend never abandoned her during those days and after a time, that friendship bloomed into romance.

When Katrina married *Walter Smith, she knew that her life was changing forever. Not only did she have a new home and a new husband, but she also had two new step-children and her little son had a new step-father. Of course, she had known Walt's children prior to her romantic relationship, but she feared that they would feel that she was trying to replace their own dead mother, so Katrina decided to go very slowly with the step-children. One reason that she worried about the children feeling like she was trying to replace their mom was that she and her little boy, *Freddy were moving into the house on Logan Boulevard where Walt's children had lived with their parents prior to their mom's death. It was certainly a delicate situation for Katrina and Walter, but they loved each other and believed that with patience and time they would overcome the pain that all three children must be feeling. After all, did not love ease even the worst of pains?

Katrina and Freddy moved into the house in 1974 and she was careful not to change too much at first. Walt's children, a son, *Jared 16 and a daughter, *Nancy, had lived there since 1970 and it had been in this house that their mother had died. Katrina was sensitive to their feelings, but she also needed to make this her home, too.

Slowly she and Walter began making little changes to the home. A new coat of paint, a different wall paper, nick-knacks from Katrina's home and more photos on the walls. Through all of this Katrina noticed that no matter what object she went to plug in or pick up, the electrical cord for it was somehow braided or entwined with other cords in the cabinet, on the floor or on the countertops. At first this seemed like coincidence, but when Katrina would try to untangle the knot of cords she could not imagine such a thing happening by accident.

She began to suspect that perhaps the stepchildren were doing this to annoy her, but it seemed like such a petty thing and the teens did not seem like petty people in other ways. Besides, would they not have done other things more directly to annoy her? She felt bad for even thinking such thoughts, but somehow those cords had to have gotten woven and knotted. It seemed like some human agency must be at work, but if not children, then who?

Ever since moving into the house, Freddy had been frightened at night. He did not like his bedroom that was the middle room on the left side of the second floor. He told her that the door to his room opened itself. He insisted that he heard footsteps on the stairs and in the hallway when he was alone on the second floor. More pranks by the teens?

One day she took the toaster to the sink to wash it up, then placed it back on the counter and plugged it back in. A little later she came back into the kitchen and noticed that the toaster cord was tangled with other cords on the counter, but how could that be? She had been alone in the house all day.

One Christmas she took out two beautiful electric candles, plugged them in on either side of the mantel and set them on the mantel. Later her stepson came to her and said that he had knocked one down and broken it. He apologized and told her that it was really not all his fault, though, because the cord had been woven around the legs of the rocking chair by the fireplace. He took her into the room and showed her what he meant. The cord had somehow been wound around the rocker. It was evident by the intricate way that it was woven that it was not an accident. When Jared had sat down in the rocker, the motion had caused the electric candle to be pulled off the mantel.

Of course, the children all grew up and moved on. By now Katrina had made peace with the idea that something was sharing their home. She was not particularly happy about it, though.

On many occasions Katrina would hear someone walking up the stairs while she was in her sewing room on the second floor. She would often call out or get up to see who was home only to find herself alone. One day she even saw the shadow of a man pass by in her periphery vision and called out thinking that someone was home. No one was there.

She would often hear someone walking the stairs up to the attic, though she never heard anyone walking in the attic. She knew very well that no one was in that part of the house, but still the steady tread of a person moving up the stairs let her know that something was up there.

There seemed no way to get answers for the problem, but things only got worse when she and Walt decided to restore the old house and put it back to the way it must have looked when it was built at the turn of the century. As she and Walt did not have the money for a lot of professionals to do the work, they decided to do most of it themselves. That meant that each day the house was filled with the sounds of ripping wood, drills and saws as they stumbled along at it when Walt had the time. Katrina tried to take up as much slack as she could by doing everything that she could during the day hours.

One day Katrina was in her sewing room working on her machine when she experienced a most knotty problem. She was using a new sewing machine that she had only used a few times before and it had worked perfectly on those occasions. Now it seemed that no matter what she did the thread continued to tangle. Every few minutes she was unknotting the thread. Finally, Katrina was exasperated and angry. "All right, I know you're there," she shouted at the air. "Now I have had enough of this knotting business. No more knotting my thread, I need to get this thing sewn!"

She turned back to her work and suddenly the machine no longer was knotting thread. In fact, she did not have to pick one knot out of anything else all afternoon. Though Katrina had been convinced of the reality of the ghost before that day, this was a defining moment for her. She was living with a ghost and it was a spirit that was both active and intelligent.

Through the years, the restoring had been continuing as they had the time and money. One job that Katrina longed to have done was to reopen a beautiful arched doorway from the living room onto the staircase so that she could see a beautiful stained glass window that was at the turn of the stairs. She could never figure out why anyone would want to cover a doorway that showed off that window. At last she and Walt decided to tackle the job of pulling that false wall down and re-opening the doorway. They began it one night, but before they got far something interrupted them.

The next day Katrina decided that she could pull the wall down herself. She pulled nails, and finally she managed to loosen the plywood that had covered the arched doorway for years. Suddenly a cold blast of air literally went through her. She had an overwhelming impression of a man running past her and up the stairs in the direction that the air had gone. Katrina felt a terrible welter of emotion surge within her. She felt sadness such as she had never felt before in her life. It staggered her and she began to cry uncontrollably. She sobbed and shook and finally she fell into a chair. Even then she could not quit crying. She did not know why she was crying, but she felt terrible sadness. After about twenty minutes of this uncontrolled weeping, she grew frightened and called Walt at work. She tried to tell him that a ghost had passed through her and that she was terribly sad, but none of that made any sense.

It took Katrina nearly half an hour to gain some control of the tears, but even then the sadness seemed to pervade her. It would take Katrina hours to gain control over her emotions once more.

After that day, the problem of knotting cords no longer was a concern. There were no more footsteps heard on the second floor or attic stairs. Katrina would become convinced that the house had been haunted by the spirit of the original builder. She believed that he had expressed his displeasure with the way the house had been remodeled through the years. When at last they pulled down the plywood that had walled up the original doorway, he had been happy to see the house restored. She believed that the sadness she experienced was the sadness he felt through the years. She told me that the icy wind had swept through her and up the stairs and out of the house.

In the mid-1990's, Katrina sold the house after Walt died and she no longer needed a big house. She did not tell the new owners of the home's haunted history. She did not want to frighten them. There was never anything bad or dangerous in the house, and if Katrina is right, there is nothing in the house now, at all. It left the day it realized that its home would be restored and lovingly cared for at last.

THE OLD WOMAN IN MY ROOM

(Duncansville, Blair County)

"It was up in Duncansville at the trailer park about ten years ago," began the young woman opposite me. She glanced nervously at the tape machine before her and gave me a smile that seemed uncertain. The young woman, a beautiful blond in her early twenties, had heard I was doing an investigation in a local restaurant and had come over to offer me her story. She kept glancing at me as if I was going to denounce her. I have seen this uncertain, almost pleading for acceptance look before. It appears often upon the faces of people who have experienced the paranormal and who think that others will call them crazy for relating their experience. I smiled back reassuringly.

"Well it was about ten years ago; I was twelve. My mom and dad had just separated, and Mom had rented this trailer and we had only just moved in. A couple nights later I was lying in bed wide-awake. I was not asleep yet." Again those eyes flashed at me both daring me to call her a liar and pleading that I would not. I only nodded and murmured encouragement.

"I was lying there when my room suddenly got very cold and I saw this old woman dressed in a long dress come in. She was very old and had long white hair. She came to my bedside and I was very frightened. I just lay there watching her because I could not move. She began tucking in the blankets all around the bed. When she was done, she just disappeared. I jumped up and ran screaming to my mom's room.

"Mom listened to the whole story, but she did not accuse me of making it up. I don't know why--maybe she had seen her, too, Anyhow, she let me sleep with her that night.

"After that night I did not see the old woman again, but every morning I'd wake up to find the blankets all carefully tucked under the mattress. My mom never did that."

The girl paused to see if I was buying her story. "We moved out about three weeks later. I never saw that old woman again, but I was still really glad to get out of that trailer."

I asked her why they had moved out. Had the ghost caused this?

"No, my parents got back together and we moved home. Still, Mom never disagreed when I talked about that old woman."

I asked her if she had any idea who the old woman was.

"No," she shook her head, "but I do know that the trailer park was put up after a lot of old houses had been torn down. I always kinda thought she must have lived in one of them and liked kids."

We chatted a few more minutes before the young woman excused herself. She seemed relieved to have told her story to someone who would listen and not call her names. She seemed to sense that I did believe her story. It was a simple tale of being touched by the paranormal and somehow it just rang true. She did not embellish it with blood dripping walls or old hags who cackle. She just described an old woman who had tucked her in. Does the old woman still haunt the area where this trailer sat ten years earlier? Perhaps we will never know the answer to that question, but this young woman's life is slightly different now because of her brush with this ghost. Now she is open to experiencing more and to learning about hauntings. She is like a survivor of some traumatic event who has to come to grips with it and who needs to understand what happened and why, before she can truly put this incident to rest. Some stories are not easily proven or disproven, but they are compelling. I thought that this little story was one of those.

WHAT'S UNDER THE STAIRS

(Clearville, Bedford County)

I have grown quite used to folks sharing their personal stories with me, but there are still times when I am surprised by them. This story that took place in Clearville in Bedford County nearly 60 years ago was such a story. Barb, the woman who confided her story to me, remembered it as vividly as if it had happened yesterday. Of course, her family had told the story many times through the years, but Barb seems to remember the impressions left by this house and her experiences in it despite the fact that when this occurred she was only four years old.

Four-year-old Barb liked living in her new home in Clearville, however, there was one thing that she did not like about this house and that was the noise. She kept hearing a baby crying loudly from the pantry under the stairs. Barb could not really explain what she heard, and to her the noise was a nuisance because she did not like hearing that baby cry. She had tried to tell her folks and her older sister, but no one else seemed to hear the loud, insistent crying, so Barb finally realized that she was alone with her annoyance.

One night her folks had some friends over. While the adults sat downstairs the children were sent upstairs to play. Barb was excited to have another little girl and boy to play with, but eventually she heard the loud crying once more. No one else heard the crying, so she tried to ignore it for a while, but at last she grew angry about the crying. Frustrated, she quit playing and came downstairs. Her mother asked her why she had quit playing.

"I can't play with that baby crying," she sulked.

Her mother's friend seemed to blanch at the child's words. "What baby do you hear?"

Her mother tried to brush over the incident, but Barb spoke up. "That baby who's always crying from in there." She indicated the pantry or closet under the steps. "It cries really loud all of the time and I don't like the noise." She wrinkled her nose.

The friend seemed about to say something, then bit off her words as she stared at the child with fear on her face. Turning to Barb's mother, she seemed unable to help herself.

"You know a baby did die under those stairs a few years ago. I knew the family and the story well. It seemed that the woman who lived in this house was having an affair with another man. She'd lock her little baby in that pantry while she went on her trysts. One day she came back to find that the baby had died in there." The woman shuddered. "It was a terrible story. They say that baby cried and cried, but no one was here to hear it or help." The woman looked at Barb in amazement. "You don't suppose that's what she hears?"

This would be the first time Barb would hear a ghost, and the first time when she would realize that she was somehow different, but it certainly would not be the last time.

She related that when she was older her family moved to another home that seemed haunted. She told me that in this second home in Pottstown her mother had a marked aversion to one of the upstairs bedrooms. In fact, her mother disliked this room so much that she kept it locked all of the time and never even used the room for storage. When Barb asked her about it, her mother could only offer a vague explanation. She simply did not like the feel of this room. Barb could not understand this attitude since she found the room fascinating. In this room she could hear people laughing as if having a very good time. This room seemed to draw her to it and whenever she could, she'd unlock the door, sneak in and play there. She felt very comfortable in this room.

The reason Barb felt comfortable in this room might be that she was a bit different than other folks. Through the years, Barb would learn that she also had another ability that is not common, and in this case, is one she wished she could loose at times. Barb has experienced many dreams that have come true. Usually, she would begin dreaming that someone she knew had died. Within days of the dreams starting, that person would actually die. Barb has struggled with this ability. Those dreams seem so real to her that at times she would announce to a close relative that someone had died. At times, her family would question her about if it were real or only a dream. Unfortunately for Barb, the dreams came true. It is easy to understand why this should be a terrible and unwanted talent.

However, there have been times when these dreams have helped her family. She reported that several times she has called one of her children and told them not to take a trip or do whatever they were about to embark upon. Each time her children did listen and it has worked out well. Once, she warned one of her sons-in-law that he should not fly because she saw smoke all around. She told him that it didn't seem to be in the cabin, but that they wouldn't be able to see out the windows because of it. This time her son-in-law did not heed her advice. When he returned from his plane trip, he told her that she had been right. Where the plane should have landed a terrible forest fire was burning. The smoke was so thick they could not see out the windows, and the plane was forced to land elsewhere.

One of her dreams also is credited with saving her husband's life. She dreamed that he had a car jacked up in the yard, that he was under it when the jack failed and the car slid off. The next day she looked out in the yard and saw the scene from her dream replayed. Panic gripped her as she saw her husband's legs protruding from beneath the car. She ran outside and told him to get out before the car slid. Just as he cleared the car with his body, the vehicle slipped off the jack. This was one dream she was glad to have had.

Barb seems uncomfortable with her premonitions, but is perfectly comfortable with the ghosts she has experienced. She has lived a very exciting life and continues to seek out the paranormal in hopes of learning more about the unusual talents she possesses.

MOONSHINE CHURCH
AND
THE BLUE-EYED SIX

(Lebanon County)

I was at a book signing in Gettysburg when I was approached by a young man who wanted to know if I had ever heard of Moonshine Church and the Blue-Eyed Six? I had not heard this story from Indiantown Gap but I did promise the young man that I'd look into it. I must thank him here publicly for offering me such a story. It turned out to be a classic tale.

Perhaps there is no other instrument of evil more pernicious than the human mind. The worst horrors perpetrated on this planet were first conceived by human beings. The story of the Blue-Eyed Six is one of those tales. It is the story of a group of men who con-

Moonshine church photo by Scott Crownover

ceived a plot to murder an old neighbor man for profit. It all began with the story of Moonshine Church and the Blue-Eyed Six, who would become notorious in the Indiantown Gap area.

Two men, drinking buddies named Charles Drews and Israel Brandt, were sitting on Brandt's tavern porch drinking beers and looking at the scenery. Suddenly Brandt saw his old neighbor, 63 yr old Joseph Raber, puttering about the shanty that he lived in with an old woman named Mollie Kreiser. Brandt watched the old man, poor and shabbily dressed, moving about the place, then turned to his companion.

"I know a way we can make a some money." Brandt watched Drews face for a reaction.

Drews was always interested in making some money. He worked as a farm hand most of the time and, though it kept body and soul together, it was not prosperous work.

Brandt quickly outlined his scheme. He and three other friends, Henry Wise, George Zechman, and Josiah Hummel had already worked out the details. They would all take out life insurance policies on the old man, Joseph Raber, stating that they were helping to support him through his lifetime with expectation of reimbursement upon his death. This was legal enough. Then they would wait a bit before killing the old man in order to collect the policies. Brandt further stated that they would each receive the face value of the policy that they took out individually, except for the money used to pay the assassins. This fee would be collected in equal portions.

Rather than turn down the outrageous plan, Drews agreed to meet the other men. After talking to the three other men, Drews agreed to join the plan. Now there were five men enlisted in this scheme to commit insurance fraud by murder. One more fellow would be added to the deadly conspiracy.

Franklin Stichler was the youngest member of the group and he was drawn into the web of murder through Drews. Drews explained the situation to Stichler and subsequently discussed ways of committing the murder. For Drews' participation he would receive $300. He spoke to the rest of the gang and they agreed to add $100 for Stichler if he helped to commit the murder.

On the afternoon of December 7, 1878 Charles Drews set the plan in motion. He instructed Franklin Stichler to meet him near the Raber house. Drews was then to lure Raber away upon the pretext of fishing if possible. However, Raber was not home the first time Drews called. Drews returned to the house a couple hours later, and this time he convinced Joe Raber to join him for an afternoon of fishing and a couple good pipefuls of tobacco.

Raber sat out upon the little jaunt without the least suspicion. The two men were joined by Stichler near Indiantown Creek. The three men proceeded to cross the creek at a narrow spot where a large board had been laid across. Drews went first, Raber was in the middle and behind him was Stichler. Stichler attacked Raber while crossing on the board and forced the old man into the water. The struggle was brief for Stichler was young and strong compared to the 63-year-old man. Stichler managed to get Raber's head under water, and at this point Drews added his weight to the weight Stichler was pressing upon the old man. When Raber no longer struggled, they finally let him up. Joseph Raber had just been murdered for combined life insurance policies that totaled $8,000.

Some of the men involved were drinkers, and it did not take long for drunken bragging of Henry Wise to reach the ears of the authorities. Suddenly, the accidental death of an old man who had slipped on a board and struck his head on a sharp rock in the stream became a calculated murder.

All six men were shortly rounded up and eventually Drews and Stichler would confess to their part in the crime. The local media dubbed the case the Blue-Eyed Six because each of the men were blue-eyed and otherwise totally respectable.

Joseph Raber's body was buried near the murder site at Moonshine Church. (The church was so named, because at one time local bootleggers would use the cemetery behind the church as an area where they would sell their illicit hooch.)

The excitement of the trials gave way to even more drama when Drews, Stichler, Brandt and Hummel were executed by hanging for the murder. Henry Wise would forever be known as the "snitch" for he had turned in his comrades as soon as he had been arrested. George Zechman was acquitted because it could not be proven that he had in any meaningful way participated in the crime. He did, however, have knowledge that it was about to be committed.

But the death of the men who had murdered their neighbor for $8,000 in insurance money did not end the story. Upon the first anniversary of the murder, people in the area of Indiantown Creek and Moonshine Church insisted that the spectral form of Joseph Raber had come from the cemetery to the spot at the creek where he had been murdered. Others who visited the graveyard insisted that Raber's specter had been seen numerous times. Certainly, if any man has a right to be restless, poor Joe Raber has that right.

Franklin Stichler's mother was devastated not only by the crime her son committed, but also by the fact that local folks threatened to desecrate the grave of her son. When a snowball bush she had planted was pulled up and stolen, Mrs. Stichler became convinced that her son's body would be dug up. In response to this belief, she had his body

Cemetery where the ghost is seen photo by Scott Crownover

exhumed and interred in her own flower bed behind her home. In a further move to protect her beloved son's body, Mrs. Stichler piled a great mass of stones upon the grave. It is said that at night she would sit up and watch over the grave for fear grave robbers were after her son. All of this slightly unhinged the poor woman, and when she began insisting that Franklin was rising from the grave folks did not take her seriously. However, through the years there have been sporadic, isolated reports of a ghostly man in the area where the grave is. Similar reports have come from the gravesites of the other three murderers.

The other three bodies are buried in local cemeteries, but Stichler's body remains where his mother placed him. Today the house Franklin Stichler grew up in has been razed and the property has been absorbed by the Indiantown Gap Army Complex. However, between a tank trail and McLean Road one-mile west of Rt. 443, the mound of stones that mark the notorious grave can still be seen.

If you do decide to visit Moonshine Church or the burial site of Franklin Stichler remember that this land is now either part of or joined to the Army facility and you must gain permission to see the burial site of Franklin Stichler. Moonshine Church, however, can be accessed without trespassing upon Army property.

WOMAN IN THE WOODS

(Franklin County)

Most of the time, I am able to give people's real names when I tell my ghostly tales. There are, however, times when it is impossible, and for this story it will be impossible. The family that confided this story to me believes that the ghost that they experienced was that of a murdered woman wrongly labeled a suicide. And if she was murdered, as this family as well as her own family has always maintained, then someone had been getting away with murder and may not want others to rock the boat. Still, the sources for this story were excellent and I was impressed with their credentials and with their honesty. I hope that you will understand why I promised this family anonymity.

For some people the topic of ghosts is a closed subject. These people do not believe in the paranormal, and they will not even consider the evidence. There are others who believe so implicitly in everything paranormal that they are gullible. These people do allow belief to get in the way of logic and reason, and that is equally as bad as being closed-minded. Most people, I have found, fall into the middle ground of being at least open-minded skeptics or of being skeptical believers. *Karen Martin was a skeptical believer. As a young girl of thirteen, Karen had experienced something unexplainable. She had been moved from her brother's room that she had always shared because her folks believed, that as a young girl of thirteen, she needed her privacy. Her new room was not a good experience for her. Each night she would hear buzzing sounds like bees in the room and see little lights shoot by her. One night she felt something at the foot of her bed that seemed to be tracing her outline on the bed. Karen had lain perfectly still, petrified with fright as phantom hands touched her legs, her thighs, then higher at her waist. Suddenly the paralysis of fear was broken and Karen began screaming and kicking. Her folks came running, but assured Karen that she had been having a bad dream. Her parents always brushed off the noises she heard, the lights and the other phenomena, as everything from an old house to imagination.

However, these experiences as a child had always remained in the back of Karen's mind and kept her questing for a way to fully explain them. She raised her children to be open-minded and questioning, and perhaps it was just as well that she had done so.

In 1995 Karen's son, *David moved back home after a tour in the Army. David began looking for a place to rent, and very quickly an opportunity fell into his lap. Down the road from David's family home there was a dirt lane, and at the end of the lane there was a trailer in which an old lady lived alone. Prior to this she had been cared for by her single son, but the son had become mentally unbalanced, and had been institutionalized. Now the family of the elderly lady was looking for someone to care for the woman. In exchange for making sure the lady had her medicine and meals, whoever took the job could have run of the trailer which meant a large bedroom and the kitchen and living room. The old woman rarely ever left her bedroom anymore and was little trouble as long as she had someone to help her with medicine and food. David agreed to the job and got the trailer rent-free.

From the very first, David noticed some odd things. His dogs would often suddenly erupt into barking as if they saw someone. The dogs all looked in the same direction and barked and growled. David could not find any reason for this. He also kept hearing a car honking its horn, but no matter how many times he'd get up to check, there was never anyone there. Now this only happened late at night and David found the whole thing very odd. Living so far down a lane, and with no other homes past the trailer, no one should be in the area. Furthermore, he never saw any car lights. David could not think of anyone who would want to harass him in such a way, and certainly no one would have any reason to harass the old woman he was caring for.

After David had been at the trailer for about a month, he had his girlfriend from where he had been stationed out west come live with him. Her name was *Lainie and Karen found the girl a bit "weird." The girl seemed to talk about ghosts and all sorts of odd stuff as if it were normal. She soon confided to Karen that she was psychic, but Karen was skeptical. She thought that the girl used the paranormal stuff to get attention.

After the young couple had been in the place a few weeks, Karen began to see some strain between David and Lainie. One day Karen asked David if everything was all right between him and Lainie. David hedged for a little bit before finally confessing. "Mom, I don't know what's going on. We've had some pretty bizarre things happen since we moved in the trailer. Stuff I can't explain and it's got Lainie all upset. She keeps insisting that the place is haunted. She claims to have seen a woman named Darla who told her that she was murdered down by the stream below the trailer and that people think she committed suicide, but she didn't. Lainie keeps insisting that this woman wants her children to know that she did not commit suicide. I'd say it was all foolishness except, Mom, at night we often hear a car revving its engine, but when I go to look for it, there is never anything there. You've been down there, Mom. You know that there is no place for a car to go except the lane and there is never anyone in that lane."

Karen just stared at David for a few seconds. She really did not know what to say to him. He could not have known the significance of what he had just said, and surely Lainie who had lived on the West Coast her whole life could not know what she was talking about, but Karen knew only too well. She had been there when the events had occurred and she knew someone in the news trade who had confided to her even more details about the events.

At that time, Karen chose to play down David's fears. She needed some time to think about what she had just heard. She wanted to think and do some research and read about the events before she went any further. She had always considered Lainie "weird" and would have written it off as just more of the same if only...

Karen went to the local newspaper and asked to see the headline pages from the fall of 1988. There on the front page was the picture of a lovely young woman with dark hair. Karen read the text. Darla McCarty (Brown) had been reported missing after she had left her husband and ostensibly gone camping in Thompson Township on Timberline Ridge. Supposedly, Ms. McCarty had been staying with a male friend in a trailer at the end of Delaney road prior to her being reported missing.

Karen flipped through the paper for the next headline about Darla McCarty. She quickly found it. The Darla McCarty Brown story had been big news through 1988 and 1989. The body of Darla McCarty Brown was found in early November by a local man who was preparing for buck season. The poor man had been hiking along the stream that ran past his property, when he had tripped over something. Upon investigating, he found that he had tripped over a shoe. Within seconds he realized that in reality he had found the body of a young woman that had been covered with fall leaves. The woman turned out to be Darla McCarty. She had died from a shotgun wound to the head.

Immediately the police were called and soon they had the entire area cordoned off. Ms. McCarty's body was uncovered and photographed. Near where she lay the police found the murder weapon, a shot gun. The body had been here for some time, but the police determined that there were no signs of a struggle and that the presence of the weapon, the proximity to the body and the position of the weapon indicated a probable suicide. The police began digging deeply into Ms. McCarty's life.

Ms. McCarty was a young woman who had two little girls. She was rumored to work as a prostitute from time to time and her relations with men, including her husband, were often strained. In fact, rumor had it that her husband was in the drug trade and often was abusive to the young woman. Darla did work as a waitress at a truck stop in Hancock, Maryland and there she often met men. She had several times gone running off with various truckers in the past, and so it was not immediately noticed when Darla disappeared again. Much of Darla McCarty's life was speculation and rumor based upon conjecture. What is known is that she left her husband and moved into the trailer where David was now staying. She had been friends with the son of the old woman David now cared for, despite the fact that her son was at least twenty-five years Darla's senior. Any speculation upon that topic would be only that.

Darla was then reported missing by her family in Hagerstown, Maryland. She was known to have been in the Franklin-Fulton County area of Pennsylvania, and known to be in the company of the son of the old woman David was now working for. Furthermore, she was found just before the end of November 1987 by a local man who was walking along the stream near his property not far from the trailer. She was shot in the head with a pump-action 12 gauge and the police suspected that it was a suicide. The police sited personal problems and her supposed profession as possible reasons why she would commit suicide. As the gun was found near the body, they felt suicide was the most likely conclusion. I have, however, spoken to people who reported on the case at the time and at least one of them told me that they felt that the case was never fully investigated. They personally felt that the police attitude was "here's a prostitute found dead in the woods from a gunshot in the mouth. Big deal. Suicide. Case Closed. No problem." Now this attitude is only a personal belief, and certainly is very critical of the local police force. I do not know what their attitude was, but I do know that the case was kept open for a while and several possible leads were followed up. Perhaps there simply was not enough evidence to draw any other conclusion.

All of this had happened in 1988 and 1989 when Karen's son was stationed out west. She had never made mention of it and, even if she or some other member of the family had mentioned the local murder sensation, it was doubtful that it would have made much impact, because at that time, David had not known any of the people involved. Furthermore, when I spoke to David he assured me that he had not known anything about Darla McCarty, or her suicide/murder until after moving into the trailer and experiencing the haunting events. He insisted that his mother had finally told him and Lainie about it after they described their experiences.

Karen listened carefully as her son and his girlfriend talked about the goings on down at the trailer. Several times they came to her with stories of late night horn honkers, motors being revved and of the dogs barking for no reason. Then Lainie began talking about seeing Darla and described her. Karen knew immediately that the girl Lainie described matched quite closely Darla's description. All of this, though, could have been coincidental or even the result of research that Lainie had done. Knowing the younger woman's penchant for drama and the supernatural, Karen had to assume that Lainie could have learned much of what she said from old newspaper archives or even local gossip. But all of that changed one day when Lainie told Karen about a conversation she had had with the ghostly Darla the night before.

Lainie maintained that Darla wanted people to know that she was murdered and that it was not a suicide. The young ghost kept insisting that she wanted her daughters to know she'd never leave them willingly. She also talked about someone taking her in a car to the woods, forcing her down by the creek and putting the gun in her mouth. She said she was covered by leaves and left there for some time. "It was so cold," the ghost said "and when they found me the man kicked one of my shoes off." Once again everything about the conversation could have been learned from old newspaper clippings except one thing--the shoe. Lainie was right that the man who found Darla had kicked her shoe off when he stumbled over it sticking out of the leaves, but no one except the man, the police and a few reporters knew that detail. In fact, it was not reported anywhere. Now Karen was beginning to believe that something was going on.

In addition to Lainie's insisting that she was psychically sensitive, and had talked to a woman with two children who had been murdered near the trailer, she also insisted that there were other ghosts in the area. She said there was a man who had been struck by a car on the main road nearby and killed. Such an event had happened in the area about two years before David and Lainie and come back from the West Coast. She also insisted that the spirit of a black man was near the creek. She told Karen and David that this fellow had died of starvation many years ago. In conversations with Karen's husband who had lived in the area his whole life, she learned that a black man had been found dead of starvation near the creek about 20 years earlier.

Karen tried not to rock the boat about this ghost business, but her curiosity was aroused. One day David came to Karen's house and he was very upset. He told her that the night before, Lainie had been restless in her sleep and when he asked her if something was wrong, another woman's voice came from her mouth. This woman insisted that she was Darla and tried to tell him her story, but he was very freaked out by the whole thing.

As time went on, this happened a second time and a third. One night Lainie literally attacked David. She seemed possessed by someone. Lainie was a small, slim girl with long hair, and she certainly was someone that David could have usually physically controlled if he had wanted to, but that night she was amazingly strong. She fought with him and screamed. When he tried to control her because she was not making sense and he was growing frightened that she'd hurt herself, he had a terrible time putting her in the bedroom. In fact, she had scratched, bruised and bit at him. She had literally ripped his shirt to shreds before he had gotten her secured in the bedroom. He had locked her in and spent the night in another room listening in case Lainie would hurt herself. She seemed to subside. David told Karen that he was sending Lainie back out west to her family. He feared for her safety and her mind if she stayed in the trailer any longer. Something there was affecting her greatly, and the longer she stayed the stronger it was growing. David was not sure if it really was this ghost, or if Lainie had made up her mind to it being a ghost and had begun to exhibit behavior that would prove her point. No matter what was the case, he wanted out of the situation. He was getting too much for him to handle.

Secretly Karen was glad to have Lainie gone. She had been disconcerted several times by the girl's apparent ability to know facts about the case of Darla McCarty and the area, but something about the girl had just not been right. She hoped that now the "haunting," if that was what it was, would settle back down now that David was once more alone at the trailer with the old lady.

For several weeks, David lived alone with the old woman once again. Once more he was plagued by the housedogs suddenly erupting in barking for no apparent reason. He still heard the mysterious horn honking late at night, and he often felt that the trailer was a bit eerie, but he tried not to let it bother him. He liked the solitude and the fact that the lane to the place required a serious all-terrain vehicle to get into the place. There was no traffic and little distractions for him. He liked that quiet after his military life. He also did not mind caring for the old woman. He sort of felt sorry for her. By now, he knew a good deal about her situation and he had learned that not long after Darla's body had been found, her son had his mental breakdown and had been taken away to a nursing home. The old woman who had relied so heavily upon her son was now forced to rely upon some more distant relatives who came occasionally to check up on her. David thought she was really a nice old person and he had no problem with her. She kept to herself and usually stayed in her room. She did not complain or fuss much and was kind to him.

Time takes care of broken romances and mends hearts. It was not long before the stress of Lainie and her ghostly visions was forgotten when David met *Mandy. Mandy was a local girl and they hit it off right away. Soon he asked her to move in with him and he told her about the "ghost" at the trailer. Mandy was not all that impressed with the ghost story, as she did not believe in such stuff.

After Mandy moved in, it did not take long for her to feel an odd presence in the trailer. She, too, heard the horn honking late at night and saw the dogs suddenly start up and bark at something no one else saw.

One evening a friend came to the trailer while the young couple was out. He decided that he'd wait for them to return because he knew they'd not be out very late. While he waited, he realized that someone was moving in the darkness near him. He jumped up startled and called out. There was no answer, but the figure of a young woman disappeared in the darkness. It frightened him badly because he heard no footsteps and no sounds.

On another evening a different friend was invited to stay over. That night the house was roused by a terrific thump on the roof of the trailer. It was followed by silence for David and Mandy until their friend came back and called out for them. He was clearly frightened and insisted that he was hearing someone talk to him in the room he had been sleeping in, but he couldn't see anyone. He was very upset.

David often confided the odd goings on at the trailer to his mother. One day he told her that the night before, he and Mandy had been playing with the ouija board at the trailer and it had suddenly seemed to come alive. He had been experimenting with ouija boards since his first days in the military and David usually had uncommon success. In fact, he had actually not used the board for quite some time because he was often too successful at calling up entities with it. That night, however, David and Mandy had decided to mess around with the ouija board for fun. The board suddenly became very active when they asked it if anyone had a message. The board rapidly spelled out the words "kill," "sex," "murder," and "water." After that night, there was a decided change at the trailer. Now the young couple often felt another presence watching them. They knew they were not alone.

As if all of the mystery and intrigue were not enough, David had another odd experience that made him believe Darla McCarty had not committed suicide. One day he was in a local bar when a woman came over and struck up a conversation with him. He chatted with her a little while before the conversation somehow got worked around to Darla

McCarty. The woman spoke as if she had known Darla, but she never actually said that she had; though she did say that she lived in Hancock. She told David, "Funny how people can die unexpectedly. Darla died because she knew too much. She was a hooker and she just couldn't keep her mouth shut. There was a cop from this area who deals drugs down in Maryland and up here. Darla knew him and she knew his secret. He was heavy into cocaine and Darla was going to turn him in. That's what killed her." After a while, the mysterious woman excused herself and left. David waited until she slipped out of the door and hurried out. He saw her pull away in a car with Washington D.C. license plates on it. It was quite an odd story that woman told, and it tallied with the story Lainie's dead woman had told her.

Through the years, Darla's family has tried to get the police to do an official investigation of the death. Several years would pass before they managed to interest the television show, *Unsolved Mysteries* in the case. They researched the story of the young woman's death and did a segment on it. They proposed that Darla had been killed because she knew of a drug deal and had threatened to tell or she had seen something or someone she shouldn't have. Though there were some leads generated from the episode, the police never re-opened the investigation.

Eventually David and Mandy were told by the old woman's family that they would have to move out. A family member would be taking their place. It was not long after this happened that the old woman was moved to a nursing home and her money and assets were gone. David, his family and his friends who experienced the haunting all believe that something supernatural did occur in the trailer. Many of them believe that it is possible that Darla did try to get their attention and appeal to them for help. Maybe that woman was murdered and she is still crying out for justice. If so, there is little hope of it. If the police were not moved by the family of the dead woman or the investigation of *Unsolved Mysteries*, they certainly won't be moved by a ghost story.

I debated long and hard about using Darla's real name not only because of the possibility of a murderer, but also because of her family. These people have been put through so much agony that it did not seem right to bring them any more grief. However, in the end, one thought made me change my mind. If this story is true, then Darla tried with every ounce of her being to let her children know that she loved them and never wanted to leave them. This might be the only way that her message of love will ever reach them. I hope it brings them some relief to know of her love. If I were her child, I would want to know this about my mother. If, however, I am wrong and it causes even a moment's grief, I profoundly apologize. I can only say that compassion was my only motive in giving her name. The story would have been just as good without it. I only wanted them to have a chance to know her message of love.

"THIS IS NOT YOUR HOUSE!"

(Brownsville, Washington County)

As much as I love telling ghost stories, I have never really wanted to live in a haunt-ed house. It would be too much like bringing your work home with you. If something falls from a shelf, I like knowing that it's because my little boys are jumping around. If my keys go missing, it's because I'm a slob and didn't put them where they belong, and if I hear pots thumping in the kitchen it is because some very real, human agency is out there mak-ing me a mess. However, for one man who wrote to share his story with me, his home life was not that peaceful where he grew up. He lived in a home inhabited by three ghosts-- and the one wanted the little boy and his family to leave!

"Now this story comes from my own experiences. When I was a kid my parents and I lived in this house located at 806 Second Street, Brownsville, and it was in this house that I learned about and became fascinated with ghosts." So began a letter from a gentle-man named Will. I read his story and could not believe how well he had adjusted to liv-ing in a haunted house as a child.

The house at 806 Second Street was a large, rambling structure, a white elephant from another era. Will's childhood was filled with odd happenings. He wrote about pool balls that would disappear from the pool table. The family would mount a search for them but without success. Months would go by, and then they would walk into the room where the pool table was and they would find them *all* neatly in the rack. At night the family would hear someone playing pool in the poolroom, but whenever they would get up to investi-gate no one was ever found.

The family heard people walking around the house, up and down the stairs, and then there was the talking and laughing that broke the stillness of the nights. No matter how often Will's parent's searched for the sources for those unnerving noises, they never found any human agency responsible. Instead, the sanity of electric lighting would reveal black shadows sliding along the walls, shadows but no people to cast them!

In response to the unnerving events Will's parents, Catholics, turned to their faith. They bought several crosses and hung them on the walls. Will wrote, "Many times we would come home and find the crosses off the walls. There were times that the crosses were inverted, and we would even find them *melted* on the register!" Apparently whoev-er haunted the house did not like religious relics.

Whoever the entities who lived in the house were, at least one of them seemed fasci-nated with the guitars and musical instruments that Will's father kept in a room upstairs. This room, the family called the "music room" because Will's father's hobby was playing music in a band. Many times through the family's stay at the house, they would hear someone in the music room strumming the guitar in the middle of the night, even though no one was there.

In particular one incident impressed Will and he wrote, "...My aunt and cousin came in from Dayton, Ohio, and were staying with us. One night my aunt heard them (the gui-tars playing) and asked my mother if my dad could not sleep the night before, so he decid-ed to play his guitar. My mother told her, 'No, he was in bed all night!'"

Most of the phenomena that occurred the family was able to explain away or just

117

ignore, but there was one ghost, the smallest one, that Will's mother could barely stand to hear. The family quite often heard a baby crying. The sound came from the porch. A neighbor would later tell them a story about a family who had lived there many years earlier. They had a baby who was about a year old and just toddling about. At that time, there was an open well on the porch where water was drawn. One day the mother of the toddler left the kitchen door open to the porch, and while she worked she lost sight of the child for a few minutes. The baby made it out of the house and fell down the well where it drowned. After that the well was filled in and covered over. Ever since that time, people have reported hearing a toddler crying just outside the house. In fact, even passersby have heard the sound and through the years Will has talked to a few folks who confided to him that they had heard the crying while passing the house. However, because she had to hear that pitiful crying of the long dead toddler so very often, for Will's mother the crying baby was the most unbearable part of the house.

For Will, though, the haunting was much more intense and disconcerting. He wrote, "The most recurring thing that happened to me was a man who would come into my room and tell me I had to get out because that wasn't my house. I would tell my parents about it, and they thought I was making it up."

For some time, Will had to endure the nighttime visits not only of the man, but also of a little boy. He'd sometimes awake to see the little boy staring at him, then the man would come in. The boy and man seemed aware of each other. Other times, the man came alone and stood by the bed and castigated the family for being in his house.

However, events would soon transpire that would change Wills' parent's minds about his making up tales. "One day my parents were in the kitchen and walking into the game room when my mom fell back. My dad asked her what had happened, and she said that someone walked in front of her and passed through the wall. From that day on they believed me."

Once Will and his mother went on a trip and left his father alone for a couple days. Upon their return, his father told them that he had a very odd experience. He had been in the living room when he heard banging from the kitchen. Will's father got up to investigate and found a pan on the stove that was making a banging sound. He picked up the pot, but it continued to make that sound. No matter what he tried, the pot continued to emit that banging sound. Eventually he just chucked it out the kitchen window because the sound was so unnerving. The pot kept banging away until it hit the ground.

Will's mother would get quite a start one day when she was on the telephone with her sister at just about the same time when Will usually got home from school. From the kitchen she saw someone pass and go sit on the couch. Thinking that it was Will, his mother told her sister that she had to go. As his mother turned away from the window, she caught sight of Will just getting off the big yellow bus. She hurried to the living room to see who had just come in, but the room was empty.

Even other relatives had experiences in the house. Will told me, "Most of our family that came to visit had experiences.... When family came into the area, they always stayed with us 'cause we had the biggest house. They usually slept in my bed because I had the biggest bed, and once a cousin of mine was sleeping with me when she woke me up in the middle of the night. I asked her what was wrong and she couldn't talk. She just pointed to the side of the bed where that man was standing telling her that she didn't belong here. I told her to tell him to shut-up and go back to sleep. Even though it was scary, I was used to it."

Eventually the family left the house, but not because of the haunting. Will, however, never forgot all of his experiences. From time to time, the family would talk about that house and what they had experienced there.

As an adult, he would take note of the house when he was in the area. The house seemed very hard for the landlord to keep rented. Will said, "It's known locally as a "haunted house." Folks rented it for between three weeks and four months usually, though it really is hard to heat, that's what made us move out, I've often wondered if it was also the ghosts."

One day Will answered the door at his parents' new home and found a young woman there. She asked him if they were the family that had once lived in the house at 806 Second Street. Will said that yes, they had lived there. The woman tried to casually ask some questions about the house, but eventually it came out that she and her family were having odd experiences in the place. "She told us that whatever spirits were in the house had 'turned violent' and had attacked her several times."

The woman also confided a single incident that convinced Will of the authenticity of the woman's story. She told him that one evening she and her husband were laying on the floor watching television while their two little boys were asleep on the couch behind them. She had just about dozed off when she heard a little boy ask, "Do you think they're still in there?" It was not the voice of one of her sons and she instantly opened her eyes to look around. Her sons were still asleep behind her and her husband was dozing beside her. Just as she was about to convince herself that it was imagination, a male voice said, "I don't know, go look."

The woman closed her eyes and slowly reopened them to find a little boy looking her in the face. She gasped and suddenly the little boy was gone. Will remembered the little boy who had so often stood beside his bed, and the man who had told him that it was not his house and he knew she was telling the truth.

The woman invited Will to return to the house and he did. He had left as a child, but now he was going back as a young adult. He was not sure why, but it seemed important to go back.

The woman's family was very nice to Will. He wrote, "One night, I was in that house (first time in years), when I had this uneasy feeling come over me. I looked up at the ceiling and told her (the current occupant) that that guy was upstairs. I went up to look and sure enough, he was right where I told her he was."

"Another time I was in that house and the guy waited until I was alone and he walked right up to me. He looked me in the face and said, 'I remember you,'" Will wrote.

It had been the violent acts of pushing, hitting, and shoving that had caused the young woman to find Will and his family, and she had also called the police. A neighbor was a police deputy and one evening when things got really bad he was called. The officer responded and found the family quite upset. Some photographs were taken and in one of them there appeared a hazy, blue mist. Will has since spoken to a local police officer who has a copy of the photos and he got to see them. Indeed there was a hazy, blue mist and he told me, "...when you looked at it through a magnifying glass it looked like a strange creature, sort of a Doberman head...nothing that was ever human."

After that family left the owner turned the building into a series of apartments. Will had friends who rented the attic. He said he only went to visit them once while they stayed in the house. He felt very uncomfortable in the attic and it brought to mind an incident that he had almost forgotten. As a child his folks had kept the holiday decorations in the attic, and one time Will had accompanied his father and another male relative up to get the decorations. However, as soon as he was on the top step he saw something dash behind an old trunk and it had so frightened him that he had turned around and gone back downstairs.

While he was growing up in the house, he learned a lot of history for the place. Originally Will's home and the small one very close behind it had been part of the same property. The family who had owned the property originally had been quite wealthy and they had built the smaller house as a playhouse for their children. It was a regular little house completely outfitted with furniture, but only used for the children's amusement. Once the children had grown up the house was used as servants quarters. Oddly, despite the many strange events that even passersby had witnessed, the lady who lived in the little house claimed to have never seen or heard anything odd.

The house has been abandoned for several years now. Though the local historical society would like to purchase it and redo it because of it's historical significance to the area, it has remained vacant. Today part of the roof is gone and the house is a derelict wreck. However, Will is certain that the ghosts are still there. He wrote about his last encounter with the house.

"In February of 2000, I was walking down this hill beside that house. I was feeling fine, until I got into view of that house, when all of a sudden I felt real sick to my stomach and really dizzy. I felt like that for a while, but when I was out of sight of the house I was fine again!"

He also described a prior event when he and his wife were walking by the house with a relative from out of town. They were only in the area because some family lived nearby and the three had decided to go for a walk. Will's wife pointed out the house as they drew near and told her cousin that it was the haunted house Will had grown up in. They continued walking until they came to the corner. There they paused while Will related some of the stories from his childhood to the skeptical cousin. Suddenly he looked up and saw the man watching him from the old music room window. He told them both to look and his wife also saw the man from an angle before he was gone.

Will's words began this story and it is only proper that they end it as well. "I think that there is more in that house than ghosts."

So who or what did Will grow up living around? Was it a ghost or something worse? Will believes that this disincarnate entity was very bad. In fact, he offered to show me the house. I suggested that I would like to bring along some of my friends who are investigators and their equipment. Will said, "You can bring them if you'd like, but I'm telling you that you won't need special equipment to see this thing. If he wants you to see him, you will see him--and this guy is not shy!"

TSHOWASZ MNYA!

(Wilkes-Barre, Luzerne County)

I have to thank Folkfinders.com for helping me locate the original newspaper accounts from the Wilkes-Barre Sunday Morning Leader, November 23, 1890.

When a badly decomposed body was found floating in the Susquehanna River between Avondale and Plymouth in an area called the Flats, the local folks did not know what awaited them. As the men pulled the body to shore, they could not know what was about to happen. This sad occurrence would spark a story that for eight years would grip the town off and on.

The local police were immediately called in and they took possession of the body. An area doctor determined to the best of his ability that the man had not been murdered. (This despite advanced decomposition of the corpse.) The probable cause of death was listed as drowning, but whether by accidentally falling into the river or by jumping in to commit suicide no one could possibly tell. The police tried to identify the man but never could. The only thing that they could determine was that he was most probably Polish, because they found some papers on his body that were written in Polish. This was scant help as they worked to give the man a name.

Eventually the authorities ordered the local poor directors to bury the body. The men who then held that position were Jim Jaquish and Bill Shupp. The two men were paid very little for this onerous job and, as no one knew who the dead fellow was or where he came from, they saw little need to over exert themselves on his behalf. Therefore, when they took possession of the body, they decided to bury it on the property owned by a fellow named Van Loon who had land down on the Flats. The poor directors scrounged up some rough boards and cobbled together the filmiest sort of box for the remains. Then they took it to the Flats near the water and dug a shallow grave not even three feet deep. There they interred the body, covered it with clay and left the grave unmarked.

However, the body would not be difficult to locate. It was only a matter of a few weeks before a heavy rain gorged the water and made it overflow the normal banks. The water cascaded across the Flats as it often did, and the clay was quickly washed from atop the box, leaving it open for all to see. For several days the box and the corpse lay exposed before the elements. Soon rumors began to surface that someone was playing a joke on folks in the area. They said that someone was dressing up as the corpse and frightening local folks as they crossed the Flats.

Other people also noticed the deplorable condition of the unknown man and they covered over the remains again. As soon as this happened, the prankster ceased his haunting of the Flats.

Through the course of eight years this scene would play out time and time again. Heavy rain, animals or other weather would uncover the unknown man's grave and soon thereafter the same person began his haunting. He was always described as wearing a slouch brim hat; dark clothing and he had long dark hair that hung down across his forehead. His eyes were always described as deep-set and penetrating, and he often approached people crying out, "Tshowasz Mnya!" in such a way as to frighten people. No

121

one would ever see the man in the distance; he just seemed to suddenly overtake them and cry out what appeared to them to be gibberish.

On nearly one dozen occasions the corpse was disinterred. At least twice the skull was actually separated from the rest of the body and hunted down and replaced. Each time the body was buried, the haunting would temporarily stop.

The situation seemed to finally come to a head on November 23rd of 1890, eight years after the restless body was first buried. On that day two fishermen were accosted by the mysterious man at a place called Buizbach's Landing. The fishermen bid the fellow "Good evening;" at which point the fellow turned and instead of greeting them began crying out "Tshowasz Mnya! Tshowasz Mnya!" The two fishermen ran from the stranger and on their way discovered that the corpse of the unknown man was once more disinterred and scattered around the area.

Finally the situation was taken before the courts and a Judge Rice ordered that the body be gathered up and a decent coffin be obtained since the first one had weathered and fallen apart. He furthered ordered that the corpse then be placed in a local cemetery where it would be safe and unmolested by the waters of the Susquehanna. This was not only a course of action long overdue, but it seemed that this was the course the dead man had long sought, for the testimony of one of the fishermen made the man's wishes clear. This fisherman spoke Polish and testified that when the ghost had accosted them it had cried out repeatedly, "Tshowasz Mnya!" These words the man translated and told the court that "Tshowasz Mnya" means "bury me" in Polish.

BIBLIOGRAPHY

THE U.S. HOTEL:

Investigations by the Central
Pennsylvania Paranormal Association

Archive Records Blair County Historical
Society

History provided by Karen Yoder

INDIAN CROSSING:

Personal interview

THE ANGRY MAN:

Personal interview via phone

Letters from the homeowner

**A HAUNTED HOUSE IN
YOUNGWOOD:**

Personal interview with homeowners

Private investigations

**THE GHOSTLY CAST OF THE
PITTSBURGH PLAYHOUSE:**

Pittsburgh Press Family Magazine
Oct. 1978

Pittsburgh Post-Gazette 1982

*Ghost Stories of Pittsburgh and Allegheny
County* by Beth E. Trapani and
Charles J. Adams III

DINGLE'S GHOST:

Personal accounts

Bygone Days In The Cove
by Ella M. Snowberger

**RETURN TO THE HAUNTED JEAN
BONNET TAVERN:**

Personal interviews

Documents at the Pioneer Historical
Society

Courthouse Records/Bedford County
Courthouse

A HAUNTED COUNTY CLUB:

Personal interviews

A NIGHT AT TATESVILLE:

Personal accounts and local folklore

Meeting of the Central Pennsylvania
Paranormal Association

PHANTOM COAL MINERS:

Personal recollections

Local folklore

Pennsylvania Fireside Tales
by Jeffrey R. Frazier

OUIJA:

Personal accounts

PERHAPS A GHOST STORY?:

Personal account

THE IRON KETTLE:

Telephone interviews with owners and Kelly Weaver

THE POWWOW MAN AND THE GHOST OF REUBEN ROCK:

Family documents of the Ferguson family

Altoona Mirror news accounts from the time

Claysburg Area Library records

THE GHOSTS OF THE FULTON OPERA HOUSE:

Interview and tour with manager

Internet records

Who Were The Savages? Massacres Across Pennsylvania by James Hostetler

Daily Stories Of Pennsylvania by Frederic A. Godcharles

OF REVENGE AND FORGIVENESS:

South Mountain Sketches by Henry Shoemaker

GETTYSBURG TOURISTS' TALES:

Personal accounts

GRANDFATHER'S SPIRIT:

Personal account through letters

THE STONEHOUSE:

Interviews with the current owner and her personal records

THE TRAGIC DEATH OF LILLIE WRIGHT SHOWALTER:

Personal interviews

Personal investigations

WHAT WALKS AT CAPTAIN PHILLIPS?:

Local folklore

Who Were The Savages? Massacres Across Pennsylvania by James Hostetler

GRAY EYES:

Telephone interview and letters

LIZZIE'S HOUSE:

Local folklore

THE TANGLED KNOTS GHOSTS WEAVE:

Telephone interview

THE OLD WOMAN IN MY ROOM:

Personal account

WHAT'S UNDER THE STAIRS:

Personal interview

MOONSHINE CHURCH AND THE BLUE-EYED SIX:

Local folklore

Blue Eyed Six by W. H. Anspach

WOMAN IN THE WOODS:

Unsolved Mysteries

Personal accounts

"THIS IS NOT YOUR HOUSE!":

Personal interviews and letters

TSHOWASZ MNYA!:

Wilkes-Barre newspaper account